A WOMAN'S EDUCATION

Jill Ker Conway

VINTAGE BOOKS

A DIVISION OF RANDOM HOUSE, INC.

NEW YORK

FIRST VINTAGE BOOKS EDITION, NOVEMBER 2002

Copyright © 2001 by Jill Ker Conway

The Library of Congress has cataloged the Knopf edition as follows:
Conway, Jill K., [date]
A woman's education / Jill Ker Conway.—1st ed.
p. cm.
ISBN 0-679-42100-9
1. Smith College—Presidents—Biography. I. Title.
LD7152.7.C66 C66 2001
378'.0092—dc21
[B]
2001033863

Vintage ISBN: 0-679-74462-2

www.vintagebooks.com

Printed in the United States of America
10 9 8 7 6 5 4 3 2 1

In memory of John

Contents

A WOMAN'S EDUCATION

PRELUDE

If we're lucky, the places and people that can give our lives an aura of magic potential enter our experience at the right moment to sustain our dreams. One generation can give another that sustenance, not so much by what they say as by how they live, and how they include one within the life pattern they've created. Invariably, the magic is rooted in place—the college lecture room, the concert hall, the perfect baroque church, the ruined temple where some teacher's words became alive, not theory but lived experience, part of ourselves. Often, as Yeats taught us, the magic is in a special house and its inhabitants.

When I married, I acquired, as well as a husband, the magic place, with resident magicians. Every summer or early fall during the first years of our marriage, we made a ritual visit to Conway, Massachusetts, to stay with my husband John's surrogate parents, Archibald and Ada MacLeish. He'd acquired them as a graduate student at Harvard in the first heady moments of 1946, after the end of the war. John was then a badly wounded young Canadian officer turned historian, while the MacLeishes were settling into life in Cambridge, where Archie had joined the Harvard faculty after spending the war years in FDR's Washington. They'd adopted the young stranger, still paper-thin from malaria and from severe battle wounds, and made him part of the family. Even sixteen years later, after we moved from Cambridge to Toronto, the routine held. Summer plans turned upon when we'd make the drive to Massachusetts, Conway, and Uphill Farm.

The MacLeishes' tranquil eighteenth-century white farmhouse rested on the curve of a steep hill above the town, so that when one sat on the lawn for tea or evening cocktails one could look way through the surrounding hills to Mount Monadnock, in central New Hampshire. The extended view was symbolic of people and place, because both MacLeishes lived for politics and the arts. Their hilltown farmhouse was at once secluded and the center of a network of men and women in public life. They saw life from what seemed to us an enlarged perspective. Archie was a distinguished poet and playwright but had also served as diplomat, Librarian of Congress, and Harvard professor, and Ada had had a brilliant career as a singer during the formative decades of twentieth-century music. So our annual visit was a way of tapping the source of the kind of creative-cum-public life to which both John and I aspired.

We'd become academics, but we didn't quite fit the mold. John's six years as an infantry officer made him impatient with a life lived too exclusively in library and classroom. My childhood on a remote and lonely Australian sheep and cattle property made it hard for me to settle too completely into an urban, sedentary profession. Archie and Ada seemed to have moved effortlessly between government, diplomacy, the academy, the concert hall. Just to hear them talk lifted the mind away from the minutiae of department meetings and budget submissions toward historic events and actors, and to great rhetoric rather than the careful expository language that seemed the academic's daily stock-in-trade. When there, I thought it entirely possible to make abrupt changes of direction in life, depending on the cause or the artistic vision to be served. Back in Toronto, and the daily round of administrative meetings, I was less sure.

I loved the journey away from the sprawling, bustling city of Toronto to the quiet of Uphill Farm, where often the loudest sounds after dusk were the crickets and where the air was heavy with the perfumes of Ada's rose garden. The drive from Boston or from Bradley Field outside Hartford provided exactly the slow process of arriving necessary to be really present. There was the drive north along route 91 to the point just past Holyoke where the Connecticut River Valley opened out into extended views of farmland and red tobacco barns, past Northampton, with the visible spires of all its churches and the bustle of a sizable market town, and then the long, flat stretch of floodplain lined with rich truck farms and roadside stands overflowing with fruit, flowers, and vegetables, before we turned off to head north along route 116 toward Conway.

Route 116 north winds uphill following the twists and turns of the Mill River, a fast-running stream interrupted by the stillness of deep-brown trout pools. The road crests just before the town of Conway, so that one sweeps around a curve of road and river to see the village nestled within the surrounding hills, a second stream broader there and racing through the town at a clip that explains why Conway became a factory town in the era of water power. Its citizens were engaged in turning out nuts and bolts for the railroads, and for the farm machinery of the early industrial revolution, until the steam engine arrived and sent the town back to its rural quiet again.

Then there was the quick navigation of the town, past its incongruously grand library, past eighteenth-century brick and wooden houses to the steep ascent of Pine Hill, where Uphill Farm sat near the crest. Arrival was always a precise moment. Guests were instructed to arrive by teatime, served Hu-Kwa tea and homemade lace cookies, and sent out for a walk with firm instructions to be home ready for cocktails by seven. Ada managed an impeccable household, with talented cook and maid, by dint of dragooning all her guests to be as unvaryingly punctual as their hosts. I studied her household carefully, intent on creating my own version of her order.

When we arrived on Memorial Day weekend in 1973, we'd barely taken two sips of our tea when Ada laid out the weekend schedule, with customary charm and firmness. There would be friends from the Smith College Music Department for tea tomorrow. Ada was presenting Smith's music library the original scores of the songs Darius Milhaud had written for her in Paris during the twenties, and a delegation was arriving to receive them. "So," she said emphatically, "wherever you go on your walk tomorrow, be sure to be back by four-thirty."

It was apparently to be a heavily Smith-peopled weekend. Friends from the Smith Art Department would be at dinner on Saturday night, along with the President of Amherst. John and I grumbled a bit as we unpacked, because we'd been expecting our usual fellow guests from the Harvard past we shared with Archie and Ada, but once we were outside, striding into the woods lining Pine Hill Road, their trees still clad in every shade of early green, the intoxication of spring quickly dispelled our mood.

The next day, we raced back from a long walk through the hills to appear dutifully brushed and shone at the tea table in the library, where the Milhaud scores were prominently displayed, and three members of the Smith faculty duly arrived to collect them. John and I, always fascinated by Les Six, and Ada's distinguished singing career in a formative era of modern music, examined them, and plied Ada with questions about their composition and her first performance of the songs. Our fellow guests seemed oddly perfunctory about the gift, and kept redirecting the conversation to the subject of women's colleges and the vogue for universal coeducation. I was an historian of women's education in North America. What did I think was the future of women's colleges? Puzzled by the turn of the conversation, I replied briefly that I thought they were excellent, as long as their leadership didn't lose its nerve. The vogue for coeducation would pass, and the record of achievement of graduates of women's colleges would become known and valued. Then John joined in to return the focus of attention to the donor and the gift. But no conversational gambit we tried served to keep the conversation on the rails. We spent an unusually long teatime discussing women's education, and then the guests departed carrying the little-acknowledged scores and uttering what seemed like inadequate thanks.

At dinner, Archie MacLeish took over, directing the talk at our end of the table to the future of Smith and Mount Holyoke and the consortium of Connecticut Valley institutions known as Five Colleges, Inc. Amherst College, the senior institution, was planning to become coeducational. Did I think Amherst's decision spelled disaster for Smith and Mount Holyoke? Bill Ward, the nervous, witty, and brilliant President of Amherst, seemed unusually intent on my answer. No, I said. People overestimated the attractions of coeducation, especially as the feminist movement was making young women value association with other women, and helping them reconsider the 1950s obligation to be paired inextricably with a male partner by one's late teens. Women's intellectual life could, just like men's, be an end in itself, and was also a valuable corrective to an intellectual tradition that had seen women's experience as derivative from a superior male version.

I suddenly noticed that Ada, the most experienced and captivating conversationalist I knew, had let her end of the table fall unaccustomedly silent as I delivered my views. The rest of the evening was taken up with the same subject, though we were used to Uphill Farm conversations ranging through poetry, current Washington gossip, the best writing of the moment.

"What's up?" I asked John, as we settled into Ada's immaculate guest room. "Those two are plotting something they're not telling us about." John laughed and said we'd know in the fullness of time. They were incorrigible about planning their friends' lives, and usually did so with splendid effect.

The next morning Archie took us driving in the black and now distinctly mature Mercedes he'd purchased with the proceeds of his Pulitzer Prize for the play *J.B.* He liked showing us the most dazzling views of the Valley and telling us the history of Conway's farms. We stopped on the Shelburne Falls road before a perfect early-nineteenth-century apricot-brick farmhouse with a Palladian façade, flawlessly proportioned flankers, a graceful barn behind, and a distant view to the apple orchards of Ashfield, lovely serried lines of trees curling over the crests of hills.

"It's for sale," he said. "You ought to think about buying it. You know you've always talked about buying a place in the Valley. And this is one of the most beautiful you'll ever find."

We agreed about its beauty, met the owners, gazed at its lily-ringed pond, and wandered through its traditional garden. We'd go home and think about it, we said.

Memorial Day brought the usual complement of lively MacLeish children and grandchildren for a ceremonial picnic by the pond half a mile from the house, where a tributary of the South River had been dammed to produce a trout-filled pond fed by springs that kept it cool on the hottest day. The routine was inexorable and delightful. Guests sat in the shade and drank potent rum punches or gin and lemonade while our seventy-year-old hosts toiled over a hot fire grilling hamburgers, just so, and laying out mounds of pickles and other treats from Archie's vegetable garden. When it was over, we would straggle up the hill, stunned by food, sun, and drink, to snooze before a therapeutic dive into the swimming pool.

As we were drifting off, I suddenly snapped awake. "John! I've remembered," I said. "Natalie Davis told me a year ago that Smith's President might soon be retiring, and that she intended to nominate me for the job. That's what's happened, and she hasn't got around to telling me. I bet Archie and Ada have been recruited to help people meet us." Natalie was my closest friend at the University of Toronto, a Smith alumna, and a distinguished historian of early modern Europe. Her words had obviously had some effect.

On the drive back to Boston the next morning, we both agreed that we were too firmly rooted in Toronto for a change, but John kept insisting that Smith was such a distinguished liberal arts college, I should nonetheless think hard about it. When nothing appeared to come of the matter, I was secretly relieved, being temperamentally hard to uproot. So except for some affectionate laughter over the scarcely concealed contrivances of the weekend, the subject quickly became submerged in the demands of my job as a Vice President of the University of Toronto, where June and July were the hot, sticky, fractious summer months when we set the University's annual budget and wrangled with the Provincial government about levels of public funding. Yet Archie and Ada and their large view of how one approached life lingered on the fringes of consciousness, and the cool leafy New England hill towns sometimes shimmered like a mirage in the desert on Toronto's most sweltering summer days.

1

CHOICE

❋ ON A STORMY DAY in November 1973, I walked back
across the campus to Simcoe Hall, the University of Toronto's
administration building, which nestled behind the dome of Convocation Hall, looking out across a spacious circle of green, toward
the amazing Victorian excess of University College, the gentler lines
of Hart House, the men's union, and the nondescript international
style of the overcrowded humanities library. The *tout ensemble* symbolized all the contradictory things I loved about the University. The
scale and classical façade of Convocation Hall spoke about the
national aspirations of Canada's oldest university. The aggressively
Victorian mien of University College announced the weight the
founders gave to its secular leanings, which opposed the church-
affiliated colleges that made up the rest of the University. Every out-
rageous gargoyle and buttress proclaimed Darwin and Spencer. Hart
House's graceful arches showed the Oxbridge loyalties that had
shaped the university's intellectual aspirations, and the overcrowded
and nondescript library announced the wave of expansion that had
swept over the university in the baby boom years. I never looked at
them all without an affectionate pleasure for the three-dimensional

11

representation they provided of the frustrations and challenges of running part of this large and untidy institution. But this afternoon my usual pleasure was replaced by exasperation at the day's interviews. I'd been reviewing the budgets of University services all day, telling everyone the unwelcome news that there would have to be severe budget cuts and personnel layoffs in the next fiscal year. Everyone knew the reductions were caused by declining Ontario government support for the University, but nonetheless the bearer of bad tidings always has to hear out the complaints of the victims, complaints I sympathized with even though I had to be firm about the cuts. It had been painful to tell my old physician friend that in his last years as head of the health service, he must scale back its quality. And the offbeat countercultural types who ran the best counseling service for youthful drug users around had looked at me knowingly as though they'd always expected that it was inevitable that I'd let them down someday.

So I didn't climb the stairs to my second-floor office at my usual pace. Still deep in thought about finance and politics, I came in the door to find my secretary poised by my desk. Petite and dark, with eyes that flashed, she was, to me, a kind of muse, her arms forever laden with mail and folders, her dazzling smile always urging me on. Though easily fifteen years my junior, she treated me with affectionate firmness, as if she were my mother.

As I signed the mail, she began rattling off details of my flight to Ottawa, who was to meet me, where the evening's dinner meeting was, all the while stuffing things into my briefcase. As she rammed the last folder in, she gave me a brilliant smile. "There's another letter from a search committee in there," she said, gesturing toward the bulging briefcase. "It's an American one. I hope you don't do it."

I was heading out the door, laden with luggage, when I stopped to ask the usual question. "Any news?" She broke into peals of laughter. "He's still there," she said, "and no one's got cholera yet." She was

Choice

giving me the daily bulletin on the determined emeritus professor who had barricaded himself in his office in the University library, refusing to move to the new space allocated to emeriti. He'd survived in his old office for six weeks, apparently without benefit of plumbing, using most of his time to bombard my office with wonderfully crotchety memoranda, which we all loved to read.

I was, as usual, late at the airport, necessitating a sprint through the elongated terminal for the Ottawa gate. So by the time I collapsed, puffing and sweating, into my seat, I'd forgotten the conversation. Then, as we waited for the obligatory deicing required by the early storm, I came across the letter from the Smith College Presidential Search Committee. Something of an anticlimax after being inspected so transparently almost six months ago. It contained an invitation to meet with them as soon as possible, signed by Robert Morgenthau, who I knew to be the much-respected Manhattan District Attorney. I glanced down the list of committee members, spotting the noted art historian we'd met in May at the MacLeishes', and a Harvard professor of Tudor history, who was an old graduate school friend of my husband's.

Once the plane took off, there was no more time to think about it, because I had to read the papers for my late-afternoon meeting and collect my thoughts for the dinner speech I was to make. Later, when I called John in Toronto to say good night and mentioned the belated appearance of the letter, he was instantly alert and said I must definitely meet with the Search Committee. I didn't want to change my life or the job I loved, but to please him, I answered the invitation affirmatively and set my disapproving secretary to work making arrangements, her cheeks pink with indignation, and the straightness of her back a powerful reproach.

The night before meeting the Search Committee at the Century Association in New York, I dined there with John's and my old friend and confidant, Stephen Graubard. Steve was a friend of John's from

13

graduate school days, a historian of modern Europe, someone who'd known me since my teaching fellow days in his and John's course at Harvard. He was an enthusiastic advocate of thinking seriously about going to Smith, or some institution like it.

"Look," he said over the Century's bad dinner and excellent wine, "you've begun working in academic administration. I doubt that you'll settle for just a history department again. You should come back to the United States. There's more to be achieved here in the private system, much more than you'll be able to do in Canada."

Steve's advice and concern with my career, and John's and my happiness, recalled our years together in Cambridge, Massachusetts, years among the happiest of my life. After dinner, we slipped easily into talk about our circle of mutual friends. His affection and friendship made it seem easier to move again.

The next day, back in one of the private dining rooms at the Century, I enjoyed the initial interview. It was a welcome change from my role as budget cutter for all the parts of the University of Toronto that reported to me. The group was pretty much what I'd meet on a Canadian governing board, but their mood was different. Faculty, the student member, and trustees alike wanted to talk about achieving greatness. How did I think Smith's pioneering history and mission could be restated, redefined, enlarged to make it *the* outstanding leader in women's education for the next quarter century? I was talking to a group of energetic and affirmative people about building academic excellence and serving the cause of women, the things closest to my heart. They seemed to take it for granted that resources could be raised for any program of excellence.

It was seductive to talk with people for whom education was *the* highest priority, rather than one in a competing set of interests politicians traded off. I began to sense the contemporary energy and drive of an institution I knew mostly from its history. The interview hummed with vitality. They were easy to talk to about my historical work, and startled by my outsider's perception that it didn't matter in the least that all the Ivies were going coeducational. I knew there were enough bright women needing an education to go around. Besides, I thought that a women's college that drew from the best high schools around the country might be a more interesting place to attend than one peopled by graduates of exclusive prep schools who might now be lured to Harvard and Princeton. We got along well.

As is always the case, a headhunter's beguiling call or a meeting with a search committee interrupts the breakneck flow of the present and sets one musing about past and future. So I went back to Toronto puzzling about where I was in life, and where I ought to be going. The question of leaving Toronto required not just the superficial check we make in a busy life to see where a midcourse correction to the current plan might be necessary, but the deeper wrenching kind of examination that goes with the decision to pull up roots and start again somewhere else.

If invited, I'd be facing a decision that would change my life course and John's. For someone thirty-nine, a move from Canada back to the United States would be more than just another academic move. It had political ramifications at many levels. I'd left Australia for the United States thirteen years before in search of wider opportunities. When I'd met and married a Canadian historian at Harvard, it had closed the circle for me to move back to the British Commonwealth world. I loved the United States and its dynamism, its intellectual drive, its passion for getting things done, but I valued the old British sense of fair play that infused Australian and Canadian political values. Stephen Graubard was right that one could have more influence from within the American private educational system. The question was one of service. Where did I belong?

Certainly the British world wasn't my only political commitment. I was a feminist, and that was a universal cause, to be served wherever the environment offered the greatest opportunity for leadership. It was a heady time in the feminist movement in 1973. But I knew feminism was a cyclical phenomenon, so one could have the greatest impact by strengthening the institutions that kept it alive in all environments, and I knew they were in the United States.

When I looked back on my life, the story of my coming of age was easy to tell. It was the story of the bright rural child carried by education to graduate school at Harvard and the academic profession in Canada. I'd met the ideal mate at Harvard. A teacher of genius, a fellow historian, a man with deep roots in my own British Commonwealth world, a quicksilver character of such charm and wit that people of all ages and backgrounds came under his spell. He was also a man of deep spirituality, for whom, as for me, art, music, and literature were important routes to understanding the human condition. I loved his effervescent humor, his extraordinary talent with words, and the gaiety that went with seeing life as ultimately tragic. And it was important that he wasn't exclusively an academic. He'd been an infantry officer in the Eighth Army in 1939–1945, and he'd grown up working summers in logging camps in remote parts of British Columbia. We'd begun our life together with high hopes and the absolute commitment that the marriage would be arranged so that I could fulfill my dream of full-time professional work as an historian.

We'd done all that. But a look at where I was in midlife called up a much more complex picture. For one thing, there had been painful, bruising losses as well as gains in the decade since I'd married and begun my absorbing academic career. The life plot I'd had in mind at marriage to a brilliant academic husband had stubbornly refused to materialize. There weren't the dreamed-of children, because I could get pregnant but not carry a fetus to term. Each set of hopes soon dashed was like having a stone where the heart should be.

And then, as my brilliant but mercurial husband's moods collapsed into long, profound, heartbreaking depression, I had something more serious to worry about than infertility. In the urgency of struggling for maturity to handle these somber chapters, I'd scarcely noticed the many possible paths opening in my professional life. But they were substantial, and the invitation from Smith's Search Committee brought them home to me in a concrete form by presenting the choice between the United States and Canada.

I could see that the Smith Board's interest was logical. I'd made my reputation as an historian writing on the history of women's education in the United States. I'd studied the historical circumstances and motives that produced the characteristic American pattern of coeducational higher educational institutions and elite colleges for either a male or a female student body. So I'd had many years to reflect on the ways educational institutions could foster or impede equal treatment for women.

And more recently, I'd become involved in academic administration. At thirty-seven, I'd surprised myself by setting aside the book I was enjoying writing and becoming a Vice President of the University of Toronto. While in that role, I could still pretend that I'd soon be back in my office in the History Department, getting ready to teach again. But to decide to become a college president would be to permit such fudging no longer. If I became president of an American liberal arts college with a distinguished feminist history, I'd have to commit to do it for a reasonable period of time, and that would involve a decision that would change John's and my life permanently.

I knew from observing the people I most admired who were a generation or so older than I that an adult life can be made a work of art. It's a slowly emerging design, with shifting components, occasional dramatic disruptions, and fresh, creative rearrangements. I thought of Archie and Ada MacLeish tossing away professional successes in the United States to live in Paris in the 1920s as poet and singer. Or some of my favorite members of the Harvard faculty, who'd changed countries for political or scholarly reasons. Now I'd arrived at a moment to scrutinize my life's design, and to decide how I wanted to develop the canvas. The process was helped by the arrival of a large packet of financial and academic information from Smith that confirmed that the job was doable, at least in the near term. Smith lacked a significant endowment, but its operating finances were in reasonably good order.

It was a scrutiny that for a variety of idiosyncratic reasons I was going to have to undertake pretty much alone. John was convinced I should make the move, but only I could assess whether this was a real calling—a vocation that would call out the best in me. In the next few weeks, the scrutiny went with me everywhere. It was the subtext of my stream of consciousness at meetings of the University's governing board, on weekend hikes with John over the Bruce Trails along the Niagara Escarpment outside Toronto, at the seasonal round of Christmas parties, while shoveling the winter snow.

My life had gone at such a pace since leaving Australia, and I had moved about so much, that there hadn't been time for taking stock or dreaming about the future. I'd been preoccupied with a freshly breaking present. Graduate school examinations, producing a doctoral thesis, marrying someone my family didn't approve of, moving to Canada, coping with John's long hospitalization for depression.

When I cast up the accounts on the matter of staying in Canada or moving into a new institution and a more public role, I thought the negatives clearly predominated. I was by nature solitary. Born on an isolated sheep station, virtually an only child while my brothers were in boarding school, I needed the quiet of libraries and the comfort of losing myself in some research project. The sounds I liked best were the subdued rustle of manuscripts and papers in an archive, and the hushed background voices of a library staff careful not to interrupt. I could manage being with people constantly, but I found it exhausting, an inheritance of a childhood where we could go months without seeing another human being come by the homestead.

Part of me didn't want to move permanently beyond the scholar's role—deliberately detached, speaking always in the third person, looking at the past from a distant present. I'd accentuated that distance by choosing to study not the history of my own country and past, where I might have met the ghosts of myself and my forebears, but nineteenth- and twentieth-century American history. This choice kept the boundary between studied and studier comfortably impermeable. Like the medievalist or the classical scholar, I wanted my knowledge to be about a world so distant one could engage it in imagination and spirit without digging around in the roots of a fragile identity in the present.

But then again, I'd chosen to study a generation of pioneering American women leaders in the Progressive era, women who made things happen to improve the lot of their sisters, women who were passionate writers and speakers on women's issues. I admired them deeply, and studying them had taught me what a woman could do with her life. But if I had a public voice, it was as a scholar, and I shied away from putting too much of myself on the line.

What I feared most concretely, with a real lurch of the stomach and a chill around the heart, was the conflict of needing to care for John either in manic euphoria or desperate depression while all my time was committed to the responsibilities and the onerous schedule of a college head in a residential community. In the privacy offered by an urban commuter setting, we could manage the mood swings together. But I dreaded the fishbowl life of a rural college community. And what was worse, being deeply committed to the fundraising event, or the highly visible public occasion that couldn't be rescheduled, just when he was in a manic spell and couldn't be found. To assuage the anxiety that goes with caring for someone who is manic-depressive, I needed to be there, to be sure to get him into the hospital, to persuade him not to undertake the foolhardy adventure, but above all to see him through the terrible depression that followed a manic upswing. He'd once told me that the onset of mania felt like firecrackers going off in his brain, and that life would be insupportable without the knowledge that at least one person understood him when that happened. It chilled me to think of not being there. And there were mundane practical considerations about dealing with a manic attack. The sufferer often doesn't sleep for days at a time, and can be unpredictably violent in emotion and action. It was wearing for the caregiver, and I knew I couldn't perform in public too well while that was going on.

John, however, was stoic and kept insisting that I shouldn't let this ailment stop me from achieving important things in life. "I don't believe in bourgeois domesticity," he'd say. "Privacy can be selfish. If you think the cause is right, we'll manage somehow."

In my optimistic moments, I knew he was right, but I still felt anxious about taking on the role of titular head of a university. I'd watched the President of the University of Toronto, who was my mentor, and had concluded that his was a pretty thankless task with very few psychic rewards and endless exasperations, since faculty and students are trained in critical thinking and are loyal to profession or career rather than institution and leader.

So imagining myself in such a role provoked profound anxiety, the sort of generalized alertness for hazard an animal shows when there is danger in the air. When I analyzed those feelings, I realized that they came from my deepest psychological vulnerability. I'd been a precocious childhood caregiver of wonderful parents who had been overwhelmed by economic and societal problems they couldn't control. I had a tendency to slip into the caregiver role and forget myself entirely, as a child does whose boundaries with a parent are fuzzy or not there at all. The result was an unpleasant sense of disembodiment, as though the self was disconnected from reality, from feeling,

Choice

from access to personal needs or wants. I'd gotten away from that predicament in my professional life, though I still lived it when needed in my marriage. What would happen to me if I got stuck in the role of universal caregiver for an institution? I might do it well but be psychologically dead inside. It was a worry I couldn't lay to rest.

John thought about such things like an infantry officer. "You're a natural leader. People will follow you. You might take a few wounds. But you're tough. You'll survive. What you should think about is what you could achieve."

When I followed his advice and thought about that, the prospect was exciting. The fashion of the moment was for the wonderful women's colleges, which were unique to the United States and a sustaining force in keeping feminist issues alive, to merge with formerly all-male institutions, or to become coeducational. Yale and Vassar were in courtship mode. Harvard and Radcliffe were moving toward merging. Columbia was eyeing Barnard, and Bryn Mawr and Haverford were considering a joint curriculum. I knew how hard it was to make a male-led university allocate resources to meet the needs of women students or to support the research of women faculty. I'd just led a year-long effort to achieve equity in pay for women faculty at the University of Toronto, and had uncovered a widespread pattern of discrimination in the process. And I knew that there was no cumulative effort to research issues relating to women, whether in law, medicine, social theory, or history. So the preservation of these institutions and their painstakingly acquired endowments was important. They were a base it was worth fighting to retain. Besides, I knew I'd enjoy the fight.

I'd been working on the establishment of a part-time college at the University of Toronto, devoted to meeting the educational needs of returning students. A very high percentage were women, and the dropout rate for them was the highest in the entire educational system. They lacked counseling, health care, time to build relationships with faculty. What could be achieved if an elite college for women began to take older women students seriously, to give them financial aid and all the services necessary to maximize their talents? What about bright mothers trapped on welfare, whose lives could be transformed by education? Underneath all these questions was my sadness that my superintelligent mother had never had the chance for an education she'd have used so well. I'd had to leave her to escape her rage and frustration at life, and her anger at me for having the opportunities she'd paid so dearly for missing. But she was the reason I'd never stopped trying to expand women's opportunities, and why I wanted to make schools and colleges treat older women with genuine respect for their intellect and curiosity.

Now that my field of research was central to the current movement for women's rights, I was saddened by the shallowness of the research base that was available to guide better social policy and political strategy. Research about women's issues was taken up when feminism was in vogue and dropped when it was out of fashion, so that cumulative knowledge was hard to develop. Now when I traveled around the continent to speak in women's studies programs or women's history courses, I saw students reading outdated work produced in the 1920s and '30s. At a women's college one ought to be able to raise endowment to support ongoing research on women, so that incremental knowledge could be generated.

Those were definitely goals to dream about. As for the traits of character needed to achieve them? Well. I had endurance and stoicism from my Australian outback childhood. I liked running things. Lecturing had taught me to be a fluent public speaker. And I loved the game of politics. I wasn't hurt by opponents or bothered by critics. A lifelong love of military history had taught me to keep my eyes on the eventual objective and not to waste time on the details of the

Choice

moment. I had unbounded health and energy and a husband who believed passionately that I had important work to do.

But I still wondered whether it was wise to choose a calling that would expose the least-well-resolved psychological issues of my life. And what if John's illness became even worse? I paid a quick visit to John's psychiatrist when I knew the invitation to come to Smith was about to arrive. "What will I do when the terrible moods hit?" I asked him nervously. "Just what you do now," he said reassuringly. "There are good hospitals down there you can rely on. I'll help you find them. You're too involved in caring for him anyway, you know. You'll have to learn to trust other people to help someday."

So when the phone call came to make sure that if offered the job, I would accept it, I said yes. It was a real gamble. But I decided to throw the dice.

2

BESIDE PARADISE

✺ W HEN I LEFT TORONTO for Northampton in July 1975, even though I knew the region I still didn't really know where I was going. I always found it easier to manage moves with John safely out of the picture. He was frazzled by disorder, and though endlessly adaptable, jittery until in the new situation. He was enjoying the late summer with friends and family on Vancouver Island until we had a house to live in and the basic things unpacked. So I had my early-morning thoughts to myself as I drove my car, crammed with family treasures—silver, jewelry, some heirloom porcelain—along the New York Thruway in steamy July weather.

It was good to be alone. I was aching with fatigue and emotionally drained. To depart *is* always to die a little, and I was leaving a very big piece of myself behind. But there was nothing for it now but to dive into this new experience like someone entering a heavy surf. I should be getting practiced at it, I thought. I'd left Australia at twenty-five, and moved from the United States to Canada at twenty-nine, and now I was on the road again a few months away from my fortieth birthday.

It was tranquilizing to have this liminal moment between worlds, with the scenery of upper New York State flashing by—Seneca Falls, the site of the first convention devoted to women's rights (a good omen?), the Finger Lakes, Utica, Albany, the bridge across the Hudson. I turned off for a good restaurant a friend had told me about, and began to come to life over a drink and a late but leisurely dinner. It was coming up on midnight when I entered Northampton. I collected the key to the apartment I was to occupy while the President's House underwent much needed renovations, lugged the family treasures upstairs, and collapsed into bed.

I'd already approved the budget for the upcoming academic year, taking pleasure in allocating the funds to launch an admissions program for older women, a first step along the way to creating an institution that concerned itself with educating all women, not just eighteen-to-twenty-two-year-olds. Smith had projected a sizable operating deficit for the year, so I blessed the Board for being willing to let me find the money somehow. Waiting for me in the president's office the next morning were the usual summer things: Fund-raising proposals—almost all inexpertly prepared. Plans for alumnae events—terrifyingly numerous and ambitious in scope. The usual crop of press interviews that spring to life whenever a woman does something for the first time. The media never look at talents, abilities, and experience—they are maddeningly concerned with the fact of being female and taking on executive responsibilities. I'd been through it all before in Canada, so it was routine.

What was a surprise was the financial picture that began to emerge as soon as I began to dig deeper into the draw on endowment and the management of endowed funds. The draw was too high, and the endowment was shrinking in value in a high-inflation environment. I'd have to get out fast with the tin cup.

I was even more surprised and depressed by the mood among faculty. In my first week at the office, every person with a grievance against the old administration, every leader in a fight among faculty, every administrator convinced Smith was in serious decline showed up to protest vocally over issues that were almost comically trivial. A falling-out among people who taught comparative literature had produced a flurry of lawsuits between faculty and faculty, some of whom, in turn, had recruited their students to file other suits.

Faculty not reappointed had lodged discrimination complaints, and each had a group of vocal supporters who crowded into my office to press their claims. Alumnae and their faculty friends were in an uproar over the design of an extension to the campus library. What was proposed *was* startlingly ugly and inappropriate for the leafy, romantic campus setting. There was nothing unusual about the disputes, but the bitterness and litigiousness with which they were pursued was surprising. I lugged home the testimony filed in all the pending legal cases and found them depressing reading. I began to wonder what had possessed me to take on this job among such a quarrelsome and complaining group of people.

But on the weekend, I settled into the luxurious guest room at Archie and Ada MacLeish's beautiful farmhouse in Conway and began to look at the beauty of the Connecticut Valley not as an occasional visitor but, like so many settlers since the seventeenth century, as someone who'd arrived to follow a calling.

The minute I was outdoors, the physical beauty of Smith and its setting overwhelmed all the doubts raised by the human community. All my life I've needed a sense of place. I can't live anywhere without finding out where I am in space and time. So I needed to know the Connecticut Valley, so central to New England's cultural and economic history, as an important background for our new adventure. The Valley was intertwined so deeply with Smith's history that both together were a source of energy for dealing with present and future. So even though the human community seemed to have temporarily gone awry, the physical place and its history were sustaining forces.

I knew the Valley was the earliest inland area occupied by the Puritans in the seventeenth century, because the river's broad expanse was their only easy transportation to the interior. But now, as a new arrival, I could see that they'd found a beautiful valley surrounded by gentle hills, about twenty miles wide where Springfield now sits, narrowing in to about five miles between more rugged hills at what is now the Vermont border.

The river's rich alluvial flats encouraged settlers to a valley created by ancient plate tectonics and the glaciers of successive ice ages. I could see the geological record of these continental events whenever I drove through a cutting on the Massachusetts Turnpike. I could look out at the Holyoke Range from the campus and imagine the last collision of North America with Africa, which had thrust it up running east to west across the valley around Northampton. Those hills had once been the height of the Himalayas, their current gentle shape created as successive glaciers turned them into the low rounded hills that now rimmed the expanse of the Connecticut River and its floodplain.

Every walk in the hills above the valley brought me into contact with the early settlers who scratched a subsistence from the shallow soil all but completely eroded from the rock ledge, many a farmer felled by the hernias that came from trying to drag the huge rocks scattered by the glaciers from fields they marked off by dry stone walls. Most secluded back roads led to small cemeteries where the hard granite gravestones told the history of families and towns.

I'd studied the demography of New England and knew that once fertile land could be reached in the new territories opened up by the Erie Canal in the 1830s, the hill-town farms were quickly abandoned, the gemlike towns on bubbling trout-filled streams remaining as monuments of an earlier era.

But the Valley continued to prosper. Its merchants were made rich by the lumber trade, by textile mills built to harness the power of the mountain streams tumbling toward the Connecticut, by the holiday and health resorts created around its beautiful scenery, its thermal springs, and its clear, crisp fall air. The humid air of the Valley summer, in which I felt hotter than I remembered ever being anywhere else in the world, eventually made it one enormous truck garden, growing vegetables for distant cities, shade tobacco for the cigar industry, and fruit and berries on the slopes of the hills, on farms where you could take your own basket and pick your own harvest.

Northampton itself recorded the prosperity that came with railroads, banks and insurance companies, and the industrial and engineering skills fostered by the Springfield Armory, an early engine of industrial design. And the surrounding Valley towns all retained examples of the beautiful, serene, and severe white wooden churches that were the intellectual center of Puritan life, many of them providing pulpits for the intellectual and spiritual rebels who pushed west to escape the rigid Calvinist orthodoxies of coastal Boston, Providence, and New Haven. There were still some of the elegant eighteenth-century houses that earned the rich merchants who built them the name River Gods. You could walk into most churches and see pulpits from which the renowned preachers of the eighteenth century had given sermons famous for their theological rigor, their learning, and their passionate rhetoric.

My longtime hero was Jonathan Edwards (1703–1758), the most famous mind and voice of the Valley, a man of such learning, his Latin and French kept him abreast of every nuance of eighteenth-century French and British thought. I relished the fact that he was an important part of Northampton's history. His use of John Locke's psychology of sensation to convey Puritan ideas about sin and damnation through vivid sensual imagery made him the most riveting preacher of his era. In his famous sermon "Sinners in the Hands of an Angry God,"* Edwards told his congregation, "It is nothing but his hand that holds you from falling into the fire every moment." And the consequences of that descent to hell Edwards described using images that every rural person had seen. Everyone, he said, had seen the spider consumed by the burning log. "There is no long struggle, no fighting against the fire, no strength exerted to oppose the heat, or to fly from it; but it immediately stretches forth itself and yields; and the fire takes possession of it, and at once it becomes full of fire, and is burned into a bright coal." His rhetoric and those of his emulators sparked the outpouring of religious frenzy contemporaries called "the Great Awakening," the first in a long line of such religious convulsions in eighteenth- and nineteenth-century America. The Awakening made a deep imprint on New England religious culture, leaving hearts prepared for God's messages and ears eagerly attentive for God's call to do important work.

My exploration of the Valley converted an abstract historical sense to a direct personal link to that dazzling past, and that link kept the quarrels and petty battles of the present in perspective. Living in a town and region with history in every cobblestone was a psychological resource I hadn't calculated into my pros and cons for the move. Jonathan Edwards's church had stood just down the hill along the Main Street of Northampton from the prosperous Dewey Farm, which became the site of Smith College in 1875. Like its fellow colleges in Amherst and South Hadley, Smith was the creation of the accumulated wealth of the prosperous Valley, wedded to the religious heritage of Puritan intellectual rigor and respect for learning. Deerfield, the farthest north Puritan settlers got by the early eighteenth century, had its Academy, predecessor of the modern prep school, by 1815, little more than a generation away from the frontier. Amherst appeared at the same time, a brother

---

* Jonathan Edwards, *Works*, ed. J. Austin (Worcester, Mass., 1808), 4:318.

Beside Paradise

college to Dartmouth, truly a seat of learning on the edge of the wilderness.

All were inspired by the ideal of the moral educational community. Jeffersonian America was anti-urban, and its colleges set in rural tranquillity were an idiosyncratic expression of an American ideal: knowledge without lost innocence—the theme Henry James, Hemingway, and countless other American minds could never let alone.

When Sophia Smith, born and raised in the Valley town of Hatfield, and spinster inheritor of a railroad fortune, came to ponder what to do with her wealth, she did so in a cultural setting in which an urbanizing America still clung to the Jeffersonian ideal but could no longer look to agriculture as the secure source of its future national character. The religious utopianism of Protestant revivals still flourished in New England, now wedded in the minds of feminists to the hope that America's women would be the saving remnant that brought the dreamed-of pure democracy into being. These perfectionist ideas were inheritances from the religious fervor of the Great Awakening and were potent sources of energy for this form of religious feminism, which flourished in New England's rocky soil.

In 1837, Mary Lyon, from the hill town of Buckland, founded Mount Holyoke Seminary in South Hadley, a stone's throw from Sophia Smith's Hatfield. The Seminary, the first higher-educational institution for women anywhere in the world, trained women in classical languages, mathematics, and science, and won support from far-flung New England congregations by promising that educated women would be the moral and spiritual resource that kept an unstable and expanding capitalist society on its proper course.

Lyon's Mount Holyoke educated the daughters of rural New England, but by the time Sophia Smith was planning the disposition of her estate in the 1870s, railroads and commerce had created a stronger sense of the nation, so that Smith and her advisers planned a college for women that would be national in scope and would rival elite male colleges like Amherst, just nine miles from Northampton, the town whose leaders produced the strong support that led Smith to make her benefaction there.

The feminism of Sophia Smith's last years was influenced by another source of utopianism: the expectation of progress, encouraged by Darwin's ideas of evolution through the survival of the fittest. Smith's dream for a women's college blended progress with Christian perfectionism. "It is my opinion," she wrote in her will creating the college, "that by the higher and more thorough Christian education of women, what are called their 'wrongs' will be redressed, their wages adjusted, their weight of influence in reforming the evils of society will be greatly increased, as teachers, as writers, as mothers, as members of society, their power for good will be incalculably enlarged."

Smith opened its doors in 1875, to offer liberal education to fourteen hardy souls who formed the first class. The timing was propitious. The long wave of economic expansion that set in for the North in the decades after the Civil War was friendly to feminist aspirations. The confident urban commercial and industrial elites of the North's growing cities believed in progress, and could embrace women's education as a sign of social improvement. So Smith grew more rapidly in its earlier years than its much older neighbor Yale, and succeeded early in raising an endowment that made possible recruiting highly qualified faculty. From these strong beginnings, it flourished as the largest American college for women, with a distinguished faculty and student body, and academic resources to rival its Ivy League brothers and its competing Eastern women's colleges.

By the time I saw it in 1975, Smith College was one hundred years old, celebrating its centennial at the crest of the wave of mid-twentieth-century feminism. The campus on the old Dewey farm had grown to 175 acres and was home to close to three thousand students. It had grown larger than its neighboring Amherst College, and larger than Mary Lyon's pioneer institution in South Hadley, and the resources of its library and museum made it possible for humanistic studies to flourish at the neighboring state University of Massachusetts, and at the fledgling Hampshire College, a new creation of the 1960s, aimed at exploring fresh models of liberal education. It was also one of the anchors of a sixth institution, a consortium of the five neighboring Valley schools, established to share academic resources and to open all five curriculums to students enrolled at any of the five campuses. All but Hampshire were inheritors of the nineteenth-century ideal of the moral educational community, a college set apart from society to foster the spiritual and moral development of the young while transmitting a learned scholarly tradition. Hampshire, the exception, combined the 1960s rejection of traditional structures of learning with the rigorous intellectual standards of its brother and sister institutions.

The Smith I came to know carried within its alumnae body the two founding utopian ideals. One school of alumnae saw the voluntarism of educated women as the saving remnant in a capitalistic society little mindful of the natural environment, the needs of children and the elderly, the prerequisites for civilized urban life. Another, not necessarily younger, saw women's education and their entry into the professions and political life as a source of progress. So Smith had established a creative program of education in social work, and graduate programs in fields as disparate as theater, music, and physical education. And it prided itself on the level of its preparation for entry into fields such as law and medicine. Between the two alumnae groups, the question of the dignity of unpaid versus paid work was a volatile subject ever ready to excite alumnae gatherings. But the vigorous and powerfully led Smith College Alumnae Association kept both schools of thought in balance and united in pride and in support of a much-loved institution.

Both groups worried about Smith's second century, because in the mid-seventies the formerly all-male Ivy League schools were all switching to coeducation, a change that many saw as threatening Smith's viability. Would it be able to attract gifted students? Would it be able to raise the resources necessary to compete with more richly endowed Ivy League institutions? Would Smith attract outstanding faculty as it had in the past?

The conventional wisdom in 1975 was that colleges like Smith could not do so, and that they must speedily abandon their historic mission and become less prosperous copies of the newly coeducational old male schools. But Smith students, freshly instructed in the value of women's institutions by the feminist movement of the 1970s, rejected the conventional view out of hand. Strong women's institutions should fight to become stronger, not give in to the fashion for coeducation. That fashion was simply the old Ivy League's response to the fact that demographic change, inspired by the idea of zero population growth, had produced a smaller cohort of college-age young in the segments of society that could afford private education.

The Smith faculty, like all good faculties, was divided over the best future for Smith's second century. It was a predominantly male faculty, ruled over by a group of senior full professors who secretly or not so secretly felt shamed that the call to Harvard, Yale, or Columbia had not come. Steeped in the ideas and values of the 1940s and '50s, they looked down on women students, while at the same time they were grateful that young women still cared about the humanities, still majored in art, music, and literature, and still hadn't deserted the humanities for molecular biology or economics.

Younger men faculty, products of the cultural upheavals of the sixties and early seventies, had been attracted to Smith by their feminist ideals, and wanted to be among those who helped educate talented women in mathematics, philosophy, or geology. Sprinkled

Beside Paradise

among the senior faculty were women scholars who were products of earlier feminist eras, strong scientists, mathematicians, literary scholars. And among the younger faculty a new generation of feminist scholars was straining to move college and curriculum toward disciplines and methods more critical of the Western male scholarly tradition.

There were questions that quickly polarized opinion among faculty, students, and alumnae. The sexual revolution of the seventies and the movement for gay rights were deeply threatening to older faculty, both male and female. Smith, like all women's colleges, had had a long history of devoted female faculty couples in Boston marriages. But these had been discreetly seemly, and never challenged heterosexual norms the way a new generation of gay women and men proceeded to do in the 1970s.

Students from smaller rural high schools were dumbfounded by both heterosexual and homosexual behavior on a campus in the throes of sexual revolution. And many parents who cheerfully expected their sons to enjoy sexual adventures at college worried greatly about the new freedoms for their daughters. So the subject of sexual mores came to complicate every generation's understanding of what a feminist educational institution should be, a question exacerbated by the society's lack of ease with all female institutions.

Most older faculty found it hard to take African-American studies or women's studies seriously. Most younger faculty were passionately committed to both. White students and black tried warily to befriend one another in an environment overheated by strong feelings on sexual, cultural, and racial politics. These tensions intensified as Smith marked its first century by its first serious effort to make its feminism encompass women of color. There had been isolated African-American women in Smith's classes before the mid-sixties, but by 1975 there was a sizable group with a strong and articulate Black Students' Association. And the centennial celebra-

35

tions themselves echoed with the early salvos of feminist scholars in the battle to insert a feminine point of view within humanistic studies, to redefine the norms of the social sciences so that women were not viewed as failed men, and to enlarge women's participation in science.

These cultural battles raged across American and Western European campuses in the late 1960s and early 1970s, but their resonance was different within the community of a women's college. American society had always nursed deep suspicions of single-sex institutions. A Protestant society thought single-sex groups redolent of popery, and likely to nourish what were darkly called "priestly vices." So the determination of women's colleges to retain their mission in the 1970s, when the fashion was coeducation, placed them far out on the wrong end of the spectrum of what was thought "progressive."

The resonance of the struggle over feminist scholarship was also different on the campus of a women's college, because it required senior male faculty to see themselves no longer as paternalistic deliverers of wisdom to young women but as bearers of a scholarly tradition that these same young women might reject. Because they were already challenged in self-image by the fact of teaching women, their reactions to feminist scholarship were the more heatedly visceral.

It was at this point in Smith's history that its trustees elected a youngish feminist scholar as its seventh president, thereby casting a vote toward one possible version of the future and setting the stage for some interesting institutional politics.

When I think about the converging lines of causation that brought me to Northampton in the summer of 1975, I'm always struck by the feistiness of a Board that settled on an Australian, resident in Canada, with a list of publications on the history of women, mostly aimed at radical redefinitions of the past, as Smith's first woman president. It would be hard to imagine a more spirited leap away from the pattern of traditional humanists from Yale, Oxford, and the University of Toronto who had been Smith's twentieth-century presidents.

But leap they did—although it took me some time to comprehend just how far they'd traveled. In any event their invitation brought me to a campus that was a literal manifestation of a century of effort to improve the lives of women. There at the Alumnae Gymnasium was the site of the first formal athletic program for women, the site of the creation of the game of women's basketball. Across the road from the President's Office was the first science building used to teach women college-level science. The crew house contained some of the first sculls used by women competitive rowers. In the archives were the papers of many generations of women reformers. The whole ambience vibrated with the energy generated by this history. And the campus, like the Valley around it, was compellingly beautiful.

Smith's central campus had been laid out by Frederick Law Olmsted, the founding genius of American landscape design. Yet another Mill River raced along the edge of the campus to fill Paradise Pond, a tranquil body of water in the heart of the campus. One looked across it to Mount Tom in the distance, visible from many points on the campus. Green and leafy as only Olmsted knew how to make his landscapes, the central campus proclaimed a powerful sense of place. There the library and academic buildings clustered around an elm-lined greensward, crisscrossed by suitably curving and uneven paths, to create a sense of mellow tranquillity.

The President's House sat on the edge of this edenic landscape, overlooking the pond and the extended view to Mount Tom. I knew all paradises have their share of serpents and that the adventure ahead would be strenuous, but as I looked out in those first months on the terrain for my new endeavors, I had no idea just how hard this particular Eve was going to have to work.

3

ENERGY FIELD

✿ As soon as I arrived at Smith College, in 1975, I began to learn that no matter how much I might know theoretically about women's institutions from studying their history, nothing had prepared me for the jolt of energy that came from experiencing one. Right in my first weeks, I found a delegation of Amazons in my office explaining politely but firmly that the crew needed new, lighter racing shells. How else could they win the Head of the Charles? And then there were the geologists who needed more money for summer field trips. These were the years of OPEC's rise and the resulting energy crisis. They needed better field experience to become good petroleum geologists. I'd always thought of women's schools, colleges, hospitals, research centers under the social science heading of "alternative institutions." But the colorful, noisy, cheerful reality of several thousand young women owning their own space, pouring out youthful energy to achieve their dreams, went way beyond such dry categories.

I realized I'd never stopped to think what the range of alternatives embodied in women's institutions were, and how they were sustained in the face of strongly disapproving social pressure. I knew in theory all about Abbess Hilda of Whitby, the famed superior of a powerful abbey that had ruled much of the North of England in the ninth century. The abbey owned extensive land, employed large numbers of agricultural workers, grazed large flocks of sheep, and administered an unruly part of England so successfully that the area increased in population and wealth. Abbess Hilda was the ruler of a large territory, and her voice sounds across the centuries with the ease of accustomed authority. And I'd read Christine de Pizan, the fifteenth-century court historian and writer on military strategy, whose female utopia, described in her *City of Ladies*, always delighted me. She pictured women building their own city, brick by brick, as a fortress within which they could pursue their own learning, free of the demand to be pleasing and compliant to men. I knew how, in eighteenth-century England, Mary Astell had almost succeeded in founding a college for women, along Oxbridge lines, her plans defeated only when the Archbishop of Canterbury advised her founding donor that communities of single women might revive popery in England.

And I was well read in the nineteenth-century belief in progress, which, along with the rise of middle-class feminism, had actually produced real "alternative" institutions for women in the United States and in England, centers of learning that paralleled existing foundations for men. But my mental picture turned out to be pale and two-dimensional compared with the complex reality of Smith, my first encounter with the reality of a century-old institution devoted to women's learning. I'd been able to imagine the books and the libraries, the laboratories and the squash courts, but not the often rowdy, mostly cheerful, and energetically political young women who peopled them.

And I certainly had not been able to imagine the political pressures, both internal and external, that constantly flowed around and within any program to advance women's knowledge base. The perpetual reporter's question was always irritatingly shallow, on a subject that would never be raised with one of my Ivy League colleagues. Was I a supporter of gay rights? If I said yes, I was assumed to be a supporter of every part of the gay/lesbian program. The next hostile question would be about homosexual marriage, or lesbian separatism. Up to July 1975, my views on these subjects had been private matters, but the second I walked in the door of the President's Office in College Hall, they became public concerns. I'd often sit in the same chair, at the same desk as Laurenus Clark Seelye, the founding President of Smith, and look up at his portrait on the wall, smiling at our mutual situation. He'd been accused of wanting to unhinge women's minds by teaching them Greek, and of destroying their fertility by encouraging women's athletics. He and I were in the hot seat where people's uncertainties about human sexuality were concerned, and always would be, because "alternatives" make people uneasy, and an institution directed at changing power relationships is always being challenged.

In the mid-1970s, it was fashionable to claim that the era of separate schools and colleges for women was past, because most elite male institutions were beginning to admit women. But two-dimensional though it might be, my historical knowledge taught me otherwise. I knew we needed schools and colleges focused on developing women's talents, and, most importantly, their ability to analyze their own experience. The coeducational higher-educational system still taught a curriculum entirely derived from male experience and expected women to assimilate to a male model of excellence.

In my college and graduate school years, I'd struggled endlessly to decide what I should define as real achievement. The conventions of the fifties said marriage and child rearing were the only acceptable female achievements. The conventions of the academic world said some part-time helping research role was about right for a woman scholar. But I wanted to see women create their own knowledge. I

thought the capacity to abstract from one's own experience and create symbolic language to make those abstractions concrete was the
major force of human creativity, and that women should direct their
own abstraction from experience. I'd insisted, as a graduate student,
on carrying out research about women, low-status though the field
initially was. I knew I needed to do that to come to intellectual maturity. Now I wanted to help build an educational system that made
intellectual maturity possible for all women.

The question was how to model such a system. I thought strong
women's colleges could do just that: be the benchmarks for the ways
society thought about educating women, be the counter instances in
physics and mathematics, or political science and economics, where
popular stereotypes decreed limited expectations for women. To
insist on alternative models was unpopular, because the prevailing
liberal orthodoxy stressed assimilation—for women, or blacks, or
any other disadvantaged group. But I knew from studying the abor-
tive history of women in the professions, from the 1890s through the
1950s, that liberal notions of assimilation had not worked. They had
been important in opening up access to professional education, but
women doctors and lawyers had been quickly marginalized into low-
paid service areas and kept outside the research base of the professions. Just as liberalism failed its believers when faced with the
economic crisis of the 1930s, I'd found in my life that the great liberal
ideal of access was valuable in giving women entry into privileged
educational enclaves—but not valuable enough, because entering an
institution (club, profession, school, military unit) did not necessarily mean becoming a full member.

Women needed their own intellectual turf, "a country of the
mind," an intellectual territory on which to stand as they observed
the world. Great medieval women thinkers like Hildegard of Bingen,
or Dame Julian of Norwich, had possessed that territory within the
powerful religious communities in which they lived. I wanted to see

the twentieth-century counterparts of that territory not just preserved but given fresh vitality.

Just a few days in the office made me see how naive I'd been in expecting that the mission of a century-old educational institution for women would be established beyond question and that my objective would fit neatly into Smith's traditions. My naiveté was matched only by the ferocity with which different Smith constituencies advanced contending points of view about how that mission should be defined in terms of twentieth-century American culture.

In its first century, Smith had prided itself on having male presidents as guarantors of intellectual standards. Nothing seemed more logical to the products of the Ivy League or Oxbridge who stepped into the guarantor's role than to recruit their old friends (naturally all male) from graduate school to the Smith faculty. So my ideal female intellectual community was taught by a faculty almost 70 percent male, many of whom saw themselves as custodians of the great Western tradition of humanistic learning, which they handed down to young women in decidedly patriarchal style. Because of their location within a women's institution, their male identity was decidedly fragile and they needed to fight feminist ideas of the academy much more than their most conservative colleagues in coeducational settings. Making sure that a new woman president didn't introduce ideas subversive of the Western male tradition was a life-and-death matter for them, and they acted accordingly.

The smaller group of younger faculty who were male feminists wanted to educate women philosophers or mathematicians to correct the male bias in Western learned culture. At Smith, the first group were colloquially known as the dinosaurs, while the second was, alas, too small to warrant a collective name.

Not all older male faculty were dinosaurs. Some were just puzzled liberals, so sure of their own good intentions toward women students that they were genuinely hurt when accused of denigrating them. Like much of the old-style left, they'd never extended their politics to sexual relationships and didn't see anything wrong with their sexual liaisons with much younger women. They continued to believe paternalistically that pats on the behind or a little fondling should be accepted as a compliment, willfully unaware that it is annoying at best to be defined sexually by someone you want to take you seriously as a mind.

The third of the faculty who were female were similarly divided generationally. The older women had negotiated academic life by two strategies. The first was to become an honorary male and espouse, with the passion of the convert, every last detail of the accepted male definition of intellectual rigor as encountered in graduate school and professional life in the 1940s and '50s. Such women were the scourges of what they took to be sloppiness and flabby minds in the younger women, products of graduate school in the 1960s and '70s, who were feminist critics of the methods and assumptions of the social sciences and humanities.

A second strategy of the older generation was to adopt the style of the upper-middle-class "lady" scholar. For them, scholarship involved exquisitely fine-grained research and elegant writing about tiny details within an established field. I thought of them as doing intellectual petit point—decorative, but working on one letter in an illuminated manuscript rather than ranging over the entire scope of a field or discipline. They were ladies first and foremost, and far too well mannered to ever challenge male authority. They were the darlings of the dinosaurs.

The younger female faculty generation had its share of honorary males and "lady" scholars, but its ranks were made up mainly of committed feminists whose intellectual energies were fed by a political vision that encompassed every aspect of their understanding of what learning was about, and which governed how they thought the institutions that transmitted it should operate.

Energy Field

But as with all other political movements, 1970s feminism wasn't monolithic. There were essentialist feminists who wanted to replace the agonistic style of the academy with maternal caring. There were doctrinaire Marxists wanting to dismantle capitalism. There were gay women intent on dismantling compulsory heterosexuality. And there were the all-too-few African-American and Hispanic women, who saw themselves as the advance guard of a juster racial society. Most of this younger generation could be mobilized around a small segment of feminist issues, but on all others they espoused radically different strategies for change. All expected that Smith's first woman president would see things their way.

In this highly charged setting, the Board of Trustees was the only counterweight a newly arrived president could deploy. I came to admire and like my Board colleagues a lot, because having cast their vote for change, they stood firm. Virginia Glover, the Board Chair who hired me and served during my first year on the job, was the ideal coach for a woman moving into an institution supported by a voluntary alumni organization. She judged correctly that if I secured strong alumnae support, I could be a speedy agent of change, and she set about designing a program to see that that support developed. She was a new social type for me, a woman who'd made Smith her career with as much serious commitment as if she'd become a surgeon or a lawyer. She was better read than I in all the publications of educational associations, and because she lived in the Washington area, she was always up to speed on the shifting patterns of support for higher education. She dressed beautifully, loved strong martinis and great parties, and was quietly effective in bridging political and generational divisions between fellow trustees. Those skills were tested in my first year by faculty alienated because of trustee determination (which I shared) to cap the proportion of faculty who could hold tenured appointments, and by a vocal alumnae group of historic preservationists who thought my predecessor's building plans were destroying the integrity of the original Smith campus. I admired and was grateful for her ability to mix firmness and a nonconfrontational style, and to leave the processing of the issues to an as-yet-untried newcomer.

Dorothy Marshall, Ginnie's successor, herself an academic, a professor of Spanish literature, a former Dean of Bryn Mawr, was the mentor who understood faculty politics and could laugh with me over the intricacies and follies of campus battles. There was not just the question of redirecting an institution run by the dinosaurs, there were other feuds to mediate in endlessly time-consuming ways. Dorothy kept me sane over the years when I had to chair the meetings of the tiny Department of Russian Language and Literature. Quarrels old long before the time of my arrival simmered beneath the surface of mundane discussions about the number of sections for the introductory language course, or who should offer the senior seminar on Russian literature, and they erupted violently over appointments and promotions. When I complained to Dorothy about the time consumed over minutiae dictated by the Smith bylaw that required the President to chair a department incapable of governing itself, her response was sardonic but soothing. "Don't worry, Jill. The last Spanish Department I was asked to evaluate was getting over the fact that one faculty member had bitten another one opposed to his ideas on curricular change. If you weren't there, they might start eating one another. So it's time well spent."

A master politician, Dorothy saw me through scrapping my predecessor's building plans to make peace with the historic preservationists, and she helped bring Board and faculty to a reasoned compromise over the percentage of faculty who could be tenured. She had a passionate commitment to academic life and its values, even though she never surrendered to any of the pretenses of the academic subculture. I needed to hear both points of view just as much as I needed her talents as a political strategist.

Energy Field

Early faculty meetings were wonderful examples of the interplay of all the competing ideological positions about women and their lives and Smith and its mission that played out in the simplest academic decisions. From my first faculty meeting, the tenor of the debates showed me there was absolutely no agreement about Smith's mission, what it should teach, who it should recruit, how it should be taught. The meetings also showed an entrenched senior male faculty determined to enforce their conservative view of learning. The dinosaurs managed to say "Madam President" in tones that made it sound like an insult. The male feminists looked astonished at their older colleagues' behavior. The "ladies" were soothingly ladylike, and the faces of the younger women faculty shone with joy that the time of reckoning with their older male colleagues was at hand. It was a sight to see from my post as presiding officer, but it often made me wish for the anonymity and impersonality of a large university. This was a face-to-face community filled with none-too-veiled personal enmities and political passions.

Shortly after we'd arrived, my husband, John, who was a gifted and wicked mimic, startled me one day by presenting me with an entire mock faculty meeting over dinner. He'd slipped in to the back of the faculty meeting room to listen to the fun, and gotten every last type flawlessly. Over the years, he perfected a dinosaur speech in which he argued with crazy logical ineptitude for an immediate doubling of senior faculty salaries, a reduction of 50 percent in full professors' teaching loads, and a return to the compulsory study of Western civilization. In the evening, whenever he saw me looking weighed down by my pile of memoranda and correspondence, he'd suddenly appear in my study and deliver yet another inspiredly zany version of the speech, each new variation leaving me shaking with laughter. An insultingly unctuous "Madam President" entered the Conway family discourse as a verb used in arguments where one party was being inappropriately condescending to the other. "Don't you Madam President me," one or the other of us would declaim, astonishing those of our audience who didn't know the code.

Laugh as we might privately over the academic politics and history embedded in faculty deliberations, there was no way that one human being, male or female, could advance all these conflicting political agendas and still keep the institution internally harmonious, or in a creative tension with the external society from which it had to draw its support. My ideal women's institution turned out to be not my ideal utopia, but a small-scale theater for the culture wars brewing across the entire range of American intellectual life.

So my new job beside Paradise Pond instantly called for every political skill I possessed. By temperament and political conviction, I didn't fit neatly into any particular cultural/political camp. A good Hegelian, neo-Marxist education had made me value intellectual conflict. I thought thesis/antithesis/synthesis could clarify the collective mind, and that—with some adjustments to make a style of intellectual life derived from the mores and life cycles of medieval monks more amenable to the realities of women's lives—the agonistic pattern worked well.

I was suspicious of the unexamined power motives cloaked within maternal styles of caring, and thought maternalist feminism politically naive. I didn't want to throw out Plato, Aristotle, and Mill just because they were men. It was true that the political tradition of the West came from societies that excluded women from politics, but that didn't mean that Western political thought didn't contain accumulated wisdom. Many centuries of Western effort to understand the question of power and its restraints needed modification to include women, but not wholesale rejection.

A product of the farthest reaches of the old British Empire, I resonated to the non-Western critique of European values, but I wasn't a sentimental enough critic to want medical treatment from a witch doctor. I knew just what kind of dentist I wanted when I needed a root canal. But I also didn't believe that these technological aspects of Western society indicated superior culture, or a better understanding of man and nature. They were like an athlete's muscles—superbly developed for the task but not so helpful in a broader range of activity.

I revered the tradition of Western scholarship, which placed me near the dinosaur camp, but I also believed passionately that that tradition needed modifying by equally rigorous scholarship about women. Not scholarship of the ladylike "petit point" kind, but rigorous, unsentimental, root-and-branch scrutiny and questioning of the categories and assumptions that shaped our understanding of the past. But I wanted that questioning to go on within existing disciplinary frameworks, because learning is cumulative, and one needs to command a discipline before one can criticize it well. That set me in opposition to essentialist feminists, who thought women's ways of knowing were different from men's. I was unquestionably in the Enlightenment tradition, valuing human reason above all other faculties. I just thought, as did some of my Enlightenment heroes, like Condorcet, that reason was a universal human faculty, not something confined to males. I was of my generation, schooled in the 1950s and '60s and not attracted to postmodern thought.

I was helped to find my political feet, and to translate what often seemed like unconventional feminist ideas, by a group of young women faculty who invited me to dinner early in 1976. They told me they thought I was being given a hard time by the dinosaurs and wanted to brainstorm with me about how to get my program moving ahead. They were a delight because of their joy in battle, their humor, their sensible feminist perspective, and their pleasure in their research and teaching. I spent so much time listening to people complain that a few hours listening to their excitement about ideas and enthusiasm for teaching became a necessary fix. I found I could trust them completely, say anything on my mind, and get the inside scoop from them on the faculty political forces I was juggling.

They gave excellent advice over dinners that were always exhibitions of culinary prowess. The group was a cross between an underground cell, a small insurgent army, a good old-fashioned dining society, and a solidly feminist consciousness-raising session. The leaders were Susan Bourque and Donna Divine of the Government Department, and Jean McFarland of the Economics Department. Joining the movable feast were women faculty from Education, Religion, Philosophy, Classics, and Mathematics. They were the colleagues and strategists I needed, and once we'd agreed on an approach to an issue, they set about building the necessary support among their peers. Without them, I'd have been a general with no field commanders and no troops. With them, the informal process of building a vision for the future and disseminating it ran smoothly. But even so, I was sometimes a puzzle to the most loyal supporters.

A lifetime of studying gender systems and their operation, and systematic reading of sexual utopians from Plato to Fourier and Saint-Simon, had convinced me that one of societies' major oppressions lay in the effort to coerce sexual behavior. We need a framework of law to manage the institutions that care for the rising generation, but that framework isn't dependent on enforced conformity to heterosexuality. I'd come to agree with the French Utopians that in a good society, men and women, or men and men, or women and women, would not have property in one another's emotions and sexual feelings. But that didn't mean that ease in dissolving marital unions would benefit women unless their unpaid domestic and child-care work were assigned an economic value. So I was close to the gay-liberation feminists, though well aware that a women's institution resting on voluntary support couldn't move too far ahead of informed opinion in the larger society on a question of unique and extraordinarily deep resonance for Americans. I understood the historical reasons for America's idiosyncratic attitudes on homosexuality. They came from a Puritan fear of sexuality, and the anxieties of a migration experience in which the male/female ratio in the population had been disturbed. Not being utopian by temperament, and also aware of the historical roots of bias, I was bound to disappoint gay activists about the pace at which I advocated change. In several respects, I didn't fit anywhere in an American political spectrum. I came from a British parliamentary tradition and thought of myself as a liberal conservative. The great British liberal conservative Edmund Burke was one of my political heroes. Like Burke, I thought institutions mattered, and that we dismantle them at our peril, as evidenced by the reign of terror associated with all major social and political revolutions. So I valued the conservative political opposition, respected it, and believed I could learn from it. These attitudes are part of the underpinning of parliamentary democracy, and they lie right outside the majoritarian American political tradition.

I also didn't fit easily in any American political alignment in my attitudes to capitalism. I thought all economic systems relative, and could imagine theoretically that there might be better systems of organizing production and distribution. But pragmatically, I thought capitalism the economic system that was able to satisfy most human wants for the majority, though it created excessive wealth and poverty at its extremes. So I could talk with the new left about the commodification of human wants, but I knew my job was to raise capital, invest it well, and generate a surplus to be invested in continuously improving a Smith education. It also meant that I didn't think people's lack of economic success indicated moral weakness, so my respect for the way welfare mothers struggled to raise their children didn't endear me to the new right.

In short, I was an ideological puzzle to almost everyone with whom I had to find a way to work creatively, and that gave me the advantage of unpredictability in the political game of running an academic institution, where the major sport and entertainment is finding the ground on which to claim an exclusive right to scarce resources in the name of the highest academic principles.

In 1975, the student body reflected the high point of 1970s feminist enthusiasm, and their joy at the arrival of a woman head of the college was more stimulating than I'd ever imagined it could be. The students came from every American state, with a preponderance from the East and West Coasts. There was a sizable group of Canadians, a sprinkling of Europeans and Latin Americans, and a growing community of Koreans and Japanese. The great majority wanted to break down the economic and political barriers of discrimination against women—be it as petroleum geologist on an oil rig, surgeon at a prestigious medical institution, woman composer, Fortune 500 executive, or record-shattering athlete, preferably in a formerly all-male sport. They were lively, fun-loving, and ready to enjoy the new experience of living with a female leader.

There were minorities of alienated women—lesbian activists, deeply conservative evangelicals, feminist religious radicals who wanted to install goddess worship in weekly chapel services—all likely to have their anger deepened by the fact that a woman leader could not (they thought *would* not) wave a wand and bring their particular utopia into being instantly. There were women from small towns in conservative communities who felt intimidated by all the feminist activity surging around the campus. And then there were the African-American students, strong, sincere, angry, pioneers in the effort to make America a juster society racially. They had to be suspicious of a woman as obviously WASP as I was, but we had a language for speaking about their concerns, because I'd grown up raging at the assumed inferiority of colonial societies and could see how condescending many liberal fixes for racial injustice actually were.

Energy Field

Smith had escaped the campus riots and angry student strikes of the Vietnam era. To my delight, I learned that Smith women had roundly refused to be organized in antiwar protests by delegations of men students from Dartmouth and Amherst. They protested in their own style—through teach-ins, vigils, special courses, but not by strikes. Nonetheless there were many rips and tears in the fabric of campus life. One saw old faculty friendships turned into bitter enmity over some position taken on the Vietnam conflict. The tiny Russian Department, which could not meet without heated altercations, was just one example of the more than usual amount of bizarre interpersonal conflicts cloaked in academic language. Students and faculty in Comparative Literature were suing one another over who could teach what to whom. A number of faculty were suing the college over alleged discrimination on matters of race, religion, or sex. Others had complained to the Massachusetts Commission Against Discrimination, which in its turn was suing Smith. The Physical Education Department was locked in deadly conflict over the square footage of offices in the new athletic building. Passions on the subject ran so high that members were playing detective on one another, trying to dig up some private dirt to advance the cause of six or seven inches of floor space! And in all these battles, each allegedly wronged party had his or her passionate supporters and critics on campus.

To someone who had spent the Vietnam War era in Canada and had lived only in large urban universities, the battles seemed easy to parody and the in-turned nature of the community claustrophobic. The rents in the social fabric were so large and visible I had an image of myself sitting in my office in College Hall with a huge darning needle trying to cobble things together. I could see that the trick was going to be to harness the effort that was now being expended in vendettas and use it for something more positive. There were enough real issues in intellectual life to generate a good fight about, without getting mired in personal warfare.

People were startled that in good old parliamentary style I didn't try to paper over conflicts but insisted that they be processed through Smith's deliberative bodies. This was in direct contrast to many preceding administrations, in which the institution had been run by an informal kitchen cabinet. That was a time-honored patriarchal style, but it was one I had no intention of emulating, even if it meant endless hours sitting listening to committees try to come to grips with curricular issues in some other way than the usual pork-barrel deal for the influential department. I insisted on talking honestly about how much new revenue should go to faculty salaries versus how much should go to financial aid in the upcoming budget, because I thought people should understand the trade-offs. And I tried to make people talk about the political battles of the Vietnam era openly whenever I saw that they were the real subtext for the discussion of contentious curricular issues.

Student affairs also needed an injection of realism as opposed to the benevolent despotism of the past. No student group seemed ever to have been allowed to fail, no matter how ill-considered the project in hand. There was always a maternal-seeming dean or benevolent president to pay off the rock band whose concert was undersubscribed, or keep the new experimental publication in print no matter how disastrously bad. I let poorly planned or sloppily executed student projects fail, as a sound education for later life. It was good for young women to be without a "daddy" who would always fix things. At first it didn't endear me to the student government, but eventually it got us on a plane of equals, with the student leaders taking more responsibility for what they supported.

I'd never enjoyed dealing with student politicians in Australia or Canada. I knew that they were using me as a punching bag to train for their later political careers and that winning was therefore always more important than the substance of the issues. Smith's student politics was fun, because it was nowhere near as cynical. Students wanted to dismantle symbolic or real patriarchy. They wanted to support gay rights, they wanted to end the notion of the college administration standing in loco parentis to them, and they wanted to claim and sometimes exercise a degree of sexual liberty, which was astonishing at the time to parents and alumnae. They were focused on work and social service and had more time for worthy causes than they had for the usual crazy student pranks. Most of all, they wanted to be taught in a fashion that took account of their being female and did not take the male as normative. In this, I was at one with them against the dinosaurs, but I was in opposition to them when they were in league with the sentimental essentialist feminists on the faculty. The argument was an enjoyable one, relished on both sides.

The vignettes of my first encounters with students that stay alive in my mind are always images of unbounded energy. It seemed as if women hit the campus and were immediately supercharged. It was dynamizing just to watch them. I loved to see women tackle body contact sports and learn how to be powerful for their size. That made me a patron of the Rugby Club, something that couldn't be an intercollegiate sport for lack of opponents. When I could, I'd go down to the field on a Saturday and cheer on the sidelines. My day was made when watching a Smith team—young, slight of body, and inexperienced—trounce a club of much older and heavier women. They were losing badly at halftime, but when the muddy and dilapidated team went back on the field, one of the forwards shouted, "Come on, Smith. Cast out fear!" They did, tackling the heavier team furiously and winning handsomely.

Then there were the people far out on the range of creative talent, who were seized by a difficult-to-realize idea and made it happen. My archetype for this kind of student discovered in her junior year that there was an important Indian tradition in which near-life-size puppets were used for performances of the full Ramayana cycle. We met because she needed money to fund the making of the costumes and the creation of the puppets. From that day, I was sold on the idea, and I waited only for its fulfillment in her senior year.

The puppets were made lovingly and slowly over eighteen months, and stored in the attic at the President's House, so that for John or me a trip to the attic for a suitcase might involve bumping into a fierce General of the Monkeys or an encounter with a ravishingly beautiful Sita. When the performance came, she'd made the puppets, created the costumes, produced her own adaptation of the stories, and somehow recruited a full cast to act as the bodies beneath the puppets. The resulting drama is etched on my mind. Someone who achieves that kind of creativity as an undergraduate may finish up as lawyer, doctor, politician, dramatist. What they keep alive in them is the permission to move beyond accepted boundaries and trust their own talents.

I am a clumsy and inept stage performer, but I always relished the parts assigned me in the senior class's review, which was performed as part of Smith's midwinter festival. The early classes at Smith had celebrated Washington's birthday, with the patriotism of post–Civil War America. Over the next century, Rally Day, named for the original Rally on G.W.'s birthday, became a proper charivari, in which all forms of authority were mocked. In the 1970s reviews, I was inevitably cast as the madam of some sleazy brothel, or the hostess in some less-than-savory gambling den, and given lines that parodied my more serious messages to the student body. My reward was watching the seniors rehearse their review, exhibiting the timeless mixture of student drive and amateur inefficiency that is the most lovable characteristic of undergraduates.

The penultimate ceremony of the year came the day before graduation, when the women who were gathered for alumnae reunions welcomed the about-to-graduate into their ranks. The ceremony took place right in the heart of the campus and involved every class gathered on the occasion in a parade reviewed by the President. One could see from the reviewing stand every stage of a woman's life parading by, from determined ninety-year-olds gamely marching, to the twenty-two-year-olds just setting out. It was a noble, serious occasion, but also a send-up of the mores of Smith in years gone by. The classes carried parodies of the popular mottoes of their day, sometimes composed with Swiftean outrage, sometimes truly comic. But underneath was the sense, inherited from Smith's first class, that this institution had broken the mold for women, and that today's graduates were still expected to do so. The parade was a literal embodiment of the field of energy created by an institution, captured and expressed in powerful ritual. I often wondered, as I saluted the parade and its slogans, what Virginia Woolf would have made of it. This was not just a room of one's own but an entire institution that its graduates owned, beholden to no one but their female predecessors. It gave women, however briefly, a sense of owning their place in life, a place never thereafter easily surrendered.

Next in power to Ivy Day, as the year-end celebration was called (after the ivy each graduating class had to plant as a symbol of their commitment to support Smith for the rest of their lives), were the Convocations that opened and closed the academic year. These had been run-of-the-mill events at all the previous institutions where I'd studied or taught, a formal ritual of low emotional valence. At Smith, they were theatrical events—electrical explosions of major youthful excitement. Everyone came, all ready to shout themselves hoarse welcoming the faculty, to sing their hearts out for Smith's songs, and to listen and applaud whatever the President had to say in greeting them.

I'm a shy woman, the product of a solitary and mostly utterly silent childhood, and by my forties, when I came to Smith, I was used to hiding behind academic robes, ambling along in academic processions, physically present but not fully there. In my generation, one was always conscious on such occasions of the male portraits on the walls, the almost exclusively male faculty, and the weight of pushing back against that tradition to assert a place for oneself. It didn't do to be too much emotionally present, because of all those ambiguities. But at my first Smith Convocation, when 2,200 Smith women began chanting, "Jill! Jill!" and drumming on the floor to accentuate the shout, I suddenly realized there could be no hiding behind a formal role. They and I were entering a little-known and rarely experienced relationship of woman leader and idealistic young followers.

"That was quite something," a male faculty member said to me afterward. "You were talking to them and I felt left out. That's never happened to me before." I understood what he meant. Our roles were truly reversed. I'd never been fully present before. I'd participated, but never with the visceral sense of leading my own kind. And previous occasions had always symbolized for him the comfortably patriarchal nature of the faculty/student relationship. I was startled by the powerful jolt of emotion the ritual delivered. I hadn't imagined it, because nothing in a modern woman's life prepares her for such an experience, although had I been Abbess Hilda of Whitby, unequivocally ruling her abbey's large territory, I might have taken it for granted. I'd wandered on to a modern version of that territory, and entered a field of force that had already propelled generations of women into enlarged and expanded versions of their lives. I could tell it was going to happen to me too.

4

JOB DESCRIPTION

✻ THERE'S NO EASY WAY to describe a college president's job, let alone explain why it's enjoyable. It involves so many often conflicting roles, played in relation to so many different constituencies, frequently constituencies with directly opposed points of view, that the result is an often laughably complex set of responsibilities. The comic element comes from switching roles so suddenly so many times in one "routine" day.

The job has the advantage of comprehensiveness. When you run a college of small to medium size, you have the oversight of all functions, the president's staff is tiny, and there is nothing for it but to learn about every aspect of operating the institution—faculty, staff, alumnae and public relations, fundraising, student recruitment, student affairs and extracurricular life, buildings and grounds, endowment management, adolescent health. You have to know and care about the lot, and you have to have a staff that is ready to do the same.

There is no title in any organization chart that captures the relationship the president must develop with the key staff, who must, in turn, help manage the relationships with all the constituencies a college president has to serve. That's especially true of the woman or man who manages one's life, one's time, one's energy, and occasionally one's spouse and family, and whose witty and trenchant comments on the ebb and flow of institutional affairs provide the subtext for the day. I used to think of my secretarial executive assistants as presiding deities, too involved in the action for the role of chorus, but definitely waving wands and directing the flow of events. When I arrived in College Hall, the team who'd served Tom Mendenhall during his sixteen-year tenure were all in late middle age, so I deliberately chose very young alumnae for my personal staff to ensure a sprinkling of youthful faces and some people who'd be learning on the job with me.

My two secretaries, Claudia Kahn and Judy Marksbury, told me when I was being foolish, stopped me from overcommitting my time, and became focal points for the informal campus information system. Erica Bianchi-Jones, who served as secretary to the Board and to the Tenure and Promotion Committee (the ground zero of campus politics), had a genius for process, which meant she saved me from inadvertent errors in administering the byzantine faculty code. She became so expert that I simply handed over all employment grievances to her to investigate and discuss with Smith's lawyers, thereby speeding the action and saving large sums in legal fees. They became like parliamentary undersecretaries, the career civil servants who made the system work. Alongside them worked the faculty assistants lured from faculty duties to oversee building projects, spearhead academic plans, run search committees, and create and hone new computer models of the operating budget. No one was ever paid enough for the time committed, so the president's staff functioned on loyalty and love of the institution.

The roles a president must play are an unusual mix of things that are usually separated by professional boundaries in institutions with public service or private profit-making missions. Or since the president dispenses administrative law, by legal and governmental roles in the rest of society. But on a private college campus, all these roles and responsibilities end up in the domain of the president, who in any one day must be teacher, manager, financial and investment expert, entrepreneur of knowledge, strategist, magistrate, and builder of warm and collaborative relationships with faculty, students, alumnae, trustees, media, and government regulators. No one succeeds at them all, and no one enjoys them all. The helter-skelter hodgepodge of playing most or all of them in one day can make the president, bringing up the rear of any academic procession bound for public stage or convocation podium, wonder, Who is this person marching along in these robes and sporting this chain of office anyway? And what's the telos undergirding all these frenetic and disparate activities? It is, of course, the promotion of the life of the mind, but that can be hard to remember when one has so little time for reflection oneself.

Because I had serious questions about Smith's trajectory toward the future, the answers to which required redesigning essential parts of the institution and redefining its external relationships, I didn't have the usual new president's honeymoon. Instead I instantly had to face the limitations of a college presidency in the 1970s. As a result, I liked being Smith's president about 40 percent of the time. The other 60 percent was utterly frustrating. But the experience was priceless—first, because I enjoyed learning how to manage this complex set of functions, and secondly because the 40 percent of the job was so emotionally and intellectually fulfilling that the other 60 percent didn't matter. The emotional satisfactions came from working with bright, very energetic people: students, Smith's legendarily loyal and efficient alumnae, trustees, talented faculty, fellow college presidents. Every day brought laughter, new insights, the pleasure of being part of a team determined to win. And in every twenty-four hours, I learned more from the traffic in and out of the President's

Office than I'd expected I'd be capable of in midlife. The job is a forcing ground for growth—not to mention character building, as one has to live very publicly with one's mistakes.

Every president is chief academic officer and must establish a strong working relationship with her or his faculty. I was a feminist, intent on making a Smith education one that gave women the tools to think critically about their own experience, and to deconstruct patriarchal intellectual authority wherever necessary. This made for some fairly fierce skirmishes with a senior male faculty absolutely determined to preserve traditions of scholarship that demeaned the female and were already being strenuously questioned in most research universities. I was working a decade or more before Allan Bloom wrote *The Closing of the American Mind*, but by the time the book came out I'd heard all his arguments before, mounted with just the same passionate conviction by Smith's senior faculty.

I actually enjoyed faculty politics, because I believed in the tradition of faculty self-governance, no matter how shortsighted the immediate outcomes. Over time, the traditions of scholarly discourse usually brought a sensible conclusion. And the tension between president and faculty was mostly creative.

My challenges were strategic from the start. A precondition to reorienting the institution was to break up or neutralize the solid-seeming bloc of senior faculty opposed to any woman's leadership. Which outflanking move would neutralize their influence? How could I change the informal rules by which the institution worked? Who were my potential allies and how might they be deployed? A lifelong feminist, I'd been in the business of deconstructing male power since girlhood. This exercise was just more comprehensive than the usual personal male/female conflicts. I blessed the old soldier friends of my childhood, veterans of 1914–18, who'd taught me to be happy fighting in a good cause, and the practice of strategy and tactics. It was comical that when I took the job, I hadn't expected to be fighting entrenched male power within a women's college, but it was just a matter of rolling up the sleeves and setting to.

The dinosaur bloc I had to break up were intent on retaining their privileged position. The ground we fought on was the introduction of feminist scholarship into the curriculum. Under their regime, it was ignored in the introductions to history and the social sciences, and slighted in literary studies. They controlled the approval of new courses, so it could have been a standoff. The solution I came up with, in concert with the lively group of young feminist scholars, was to offer a countercurriculum scheduled to be delivered in between sessions of the major core courses, so that students who flocked to classes taught by the President and her allies carried their own feminist curriculum into the faculty-approved classroom. No curriculum committee could constrain voluntary teaching for which no credit was claimed, even though the extra classes changed what went on in the classroom. After some months of searching student criticism, the old guard caved and let it be known they'd approve feminist scholarship in formal courses.

A president doesn't control the curriculum, a cherished faculty prerogative, but she does control the incentive system offered to support research. I found a chance to introduce strong incentives for research on women through the help of the president of the Andrew W. Mellon Foundation, who always asked new presidents in liberal arts colleges what support they needed to make their leadership more effective. He was startled when my response was that I wanted funding to support research and teaching about women's experience across the humanities and social sciences. He even called the day before his board was to vote the grant to make sure I had no second thoughts or worries about the enemies that the introduction of so overtly feminist a program would make. I said I had none, because these were the kind of enemies I enjoyed making.

The grant meant that any Smith faculty member who wanted to

embrace the new scholarship could find released time to develop her or his teaching and research, including travel money and summer salaries. I'd made no frontal attack on entrenched conservative opinion. It had simply been outflanked. Over time, the incentive system worked without a blow being struck. Moreover, the results of the new research could be widely reported, constituting another kind of teaching, which academic respect for freedom of expression made it impossible to constrain. Best of all, the fight led me to a lively set of colleagues who kept me in touch with advanced research on women.

In fact, the newly funded research program, known as the Project on Women and Social Change, helped keep my scholarly life going despite the presidency. It held its first summer conference on the subject of women's autobiography, the issue beginning to concern me as a question that fell between literary and historical studies. The papers gave me a literary perspective on a subject I knew as an historian and set me thinking in new ways about my own inner-life narrative. So the public fight ended up enriching my private intellectual life.

But even as the curriculum content was being changed, there were still endless procedural debates to negotiate. It's hard to convey the sleepy snail's pace at which faculty debates proceed. I'd been astonished on arriving at Smith to discover that accounting was taught in heavily oversubscribed courses for which credit was not given. Why was that? I was told with patient condescension, "Because accounting is not a traditional liberal arts subject." It didn't matter that the entire constellation of liberal arts schools established for men surrounding us gave credit for accounting. Women should be pure, even if unemployable. It took eighteen months of committee discussion and faculty deliberation to change something self-evidently necessary to a woman who'd had to teach herself how to read a balance sheet in order to run institutions.

Of course I understood that the pace of faculty deliberations was dictated by the academic's wish to be left alone to think about her or his specialty and to teach it to the ideal student, leaving it to a president and her or his administrative team to raise the money to make this possible under the most favorable circumstances. In practice, however, the faculty doesn't trust the president to do this, while the president can only succeed in securing the best possible circumstances for the institution if she or he is able to bring what the faculty want to do into some creative relationship with the needs of students and the interests of society, which must support the enterprise. This might seem like a simple task, but since the faculty controls the curriculum, and the tenuring of permanent faculty members, it requires persuasion of a high order to bring about what can seem like glacial rates of change. The difficulty of getting traction on change was exacerbated at Smith because of the faculty demography. A high percentage were in their late fifties and early sixties, people intent on preserving the ideals of their graduate initiation into the profession, when scorn for business skills such as accounting was a hangover from the Depression era, and when the study of women was not a serious intellectual concern.

I quickly realized that a president's relationship to a faculty involves more double binds than a bad marriage on the brink of collapse. While not trusting the president, the faculty also expects her or him to be omnipotent in securing its particular goals. The result is that most presidents are scapegoats for the inevitable disappointments of scholarly life, and they listen to more complaining than affirmation. If the faculty is aging, as Smith's was in the seventies, the recurring refrain is that "students today are not what they once were, standards are slipping, and the institution is going to the dogs." And it would have been tactless to point out that the complainers were more exciting to students when in the first flush of their scholarly careers than they had now become.

But for every dozen or so visitors who came to talk about not being "happy" about their life in the institution, there would be the one scholar who came in to talk about the new discovery aided by the much cherished new equipment, or improved library, or chance for study-leave that changed his or her life, made possible a new insight, opened up new questions, and it was those meetings that counted. As I worked at raising the funding to support faculty research, those meetings became more frequent and more rewarding.

If the faculty relationship, for systemic reasons, is always problematic, the alumnae relationship is exactly the opposite. Smith women were, to me, a constant validation of the institution. Wherever I went across the United States or in Europe, they were the builders of institutions, models of engagement in civic and cultural life, leaders of environmental preservation. In the 1970s, they were eager to work with a woman leader, and to support a redefinition of Smith's educational mission in line with the realities of contemporary women's working lives and career aspirations. Whatever their age and circumstances, they wanted to give time, energy, resources to an institution that had given them the chance to live in a female-directed world during a crucial stage of their lives. Faculty might be bearers of old attitudes, but the experience of self-governing women's communities that existed in Smith's thirty-eight houses had prepared alumnae to run organizations and manage their environment. They ran such a well-tuned support organization that I enjoyed my itinerant life as a fundraiser intensely. It was good that I did, because since the faculty was almost fully tenured, I could change Smith's culture only by raising new resources, introducing new fields, bringing senior women scholars to the faculty, supporting competitive athletics. The asking was fun, and my first national fund drive was a big piece of the 40 percent of the job that I loved.

A national fund drive is just like a political campaign. Because of the talent for organization and the pleasure in working with other Smith women that come from life in a women's college, fundraising travels for Smith are a blast. You have a map in your mind's eye of where the support is strongest, where it's wavering, where there is strong leadership, where the organization is adrift. Whatever the campaign event of the day, the routine is predictable. You emerge from the plane to meet a smiling delegation of unmistakably Smith women—identifiable by their obvious pleasure in the task of the moment, their disciplined sense that no detail in the day's plan has been left untended, and their obvious pleasure that there would shortly be a great celebration of Smith in the context of exciting new plans for its future.

With this attitude, campaign events were splendid parties, flawlessly executed by skilled hostesses. They hummed with energy and enthusiasm, and every single person in the room wanted to meet the new President. I loved talking about women's education in this setting where there wasn't a naysayer in the bunch. And even when the campaign plans called for two or three weeks of such occasions, they were run with such panache that I couldn't get tired. John Conway, who often accompanied me, could never stop marveling at the spit and polish of Smith's nonmilitary army. He'd been an infantry officer in the legendary Eighth Army in the Second World War, wading ashore in the first wave of the invasions of Sicily and Italy. He always said he wished Smith alumnae had been in charge of the logistics of both invasions, because without question, things would have gone a lot more smoothly.

The electric identification between woman president and female alumnae body also fed my psychic energy. In the modern world, a woman doesn't often feel that she has 40,000-plus loyal followers ready—indeed, eager—to fall in behind the goal of the moment. Even older alumnae who'd loved their fatherly academic mentors, most especially Smith's beloved President William Allan Neilson, would come up to me to say, "I'm of my generation, and I was disappointed when we didn't appoint another male president. Someone as wonderful as President Neilson. But I was wrong. I just couldn't imagine what it would be like to have a woman leader. Now I can. You can call on me for anything it's in my power to do. I was never prouder of Smith." The generous response was a blessing, but also a strange new experience. I'd thought about doing a professional job. But here I was being given a mission that went way beyond my standard professional training to who I was personally and how I related to these wonderful people. It was sobering and exhilarating at the same time. I was used to my parents' ghosts inhabiting my psyche with compelling demands for high performance, but I'd suddenly acquired 40,000 other friendly people with equally strong expectations. I'd spent my young adult years carefully creating the detached identity of the professional scholar. It was hard to abandon that façade and become a person people identified with emotionally. These great meetings along the campaign trail forced me to think harder about who I was and what I was bringing to the job. It was no longer a matter of the right scholarly footnotes. The question had become what emotional range and power I could muster to call out the best from this large and distinguished alumnae body. And there was no escaping it.

I found meeting donors face to face endlessly fascinating. One entered their lives when what was uppermost in their minds was their wealth and how to use it wisely. Conversations about gifts to Smith always led into the heart of a family, its generations, its black sheep, its golden boys and girls, and the donor's youthful dreams, all weighed against the realities of the present. I found the meetings like stepping between the pages of a George Eliot novel, or any one of the great Victorian family sagas. On rare occasions the mood and pace of the relationship recalled Proust, but always I found myself learning a lot from the reasons why. I often felt Henry James walking beside me, explaining the complexities of the family of the moment with such artistry that asking was no problem. But the mere fact of doing it carried me into many close relationships with a range and variety of people I would otherwise never have met. Up until my arrival at Smith, I'd lived in a comfortable world of like-minded academics. Suddenly I was just as likely to be in daily discussions with founders of the John Birch Society, utopian leftists, capitalists who thought Thomas Jefferson too left-leaning, hardy old New Dealers who thought Roosevelt should have listened more to Wallace, people from every facet of American wealth and political persuasion. They made my study of American social history three-dimensional and gave me an invaluable education. I was always stimulated, amused, and instructed by the people I met. And I found myself forming important new friendships long past the age when one expects to do so.

After I'd given my advice about family matters and we'd settled on the gift for Smith, I usually got some advice given to me. It could vary from where to get the best facelift at what age, to how to care for "that nice husband of yours" properly, to hot tips on the stock market, to advice about dress. "Don't wear black. It always ages a woman. Even if you have really good diamonds to go with it."

Whatever the group, and the nature of the advice, the learning was fun. Women old enough to be my mother told me about the experience of volunteer relief work in Europe in the First World War. Their humor and laughter about being the first women to take on such tasks gave a time perspective to my life that was priceless. Older women volunteers who'd set about improving a city's schools, or rescuing the tidal marshes of a coastline, or building a museum taught me about voluntary organizations. And the young women professionals—surgeons, geologists, elected officials—pushing at the boundaries of women's careers were tireless in supporting my aim to connect Smith women's undergraduate experience with professional life after graduation. I fell asleep at night and woke up in the morning feeling stronger just for knowing them all.

Smith's 1977–79 campaign raised the capital we needed to

recover some of the ground lost in Smith's endowment during the high-inflation years of the 1970s, and it enabled much-needed investment in plant renovation and expansion. But most importantly, it built Smith's fundraising capacity so that we continued raising capital annually at the rate set by the best years of the fund drive.

But although our fundraising was successful, the poor performance of our endowment managers meant that I and my volunteer fundraising team were pouring money into a leaky bucket, a disastrous course in a period of high inflation. Having always lived in publicly funded institutions, and having left the management of my own retirement funds to the venerable Teachers Insurance and Annuity Association, I hadn't paid much attention to money management. Now it was clear I needed to learn about it fast.

An Australian outback childhood, where all problems had to be solved without the assistance of experts, meant that I assumed I could learn what I needed to know to deal with almost any problem. It was clear I needed to find someone to teach me how to assess money managers and portfolio strategies. I asked Smith's knowledgeable chief financial officer who in Smith's network could teach me money management. His answer was instantaneous. Al Gordon, the Chairman of Kidder Peabody, had served as a Smith trustee and was the husband, brother, and father of loyal and distinguished Smith women. I called him up, asked for a reading list, and made a date for my first tutorial.

I had found one of Wall Street's grand old men to be my teacher. He was as good an instructor as he was a financier, and before long I was able to argue energetically with Smith's investment committee that the time had come to make a change in managers and rethink our investment strategy. I had, as ally, another legendary figure, this time from the pension world. Roger Murray, a Columbia Business School professor and Smith trustee, was champing at the bit to make a change but hadn't been able to shift a cautious committee.

He and I were pushing for more professional management, while the committee and its fellow trustees had in mind that Dwight Morrow, one of Smith's largest donors, had been J. P. Morgan's partner, which was how Smith's long relationship with the Morgan Bank had begun. The trustees thought it a connection not to be discarded lightly. Our relationship was certainly clubby, and very amiable. The menus at our quarterly meetings were always splendid. But we were losing money, quarter after quarter, because of a misguided investment strategy.

At last the day came when the committee agreed that the time had come to inform our advisers that if the performance didn't improve, a change had to be made. Roger Murray and I were assigned to call and deliver the message together. When the appointed hour arrived, there was a winter blizzard. Roger's plane was canceled, so I had to make the call alone. I almost never had flashbacks to my childhood in rural Australia, but on this occasion, as the cab deposited me at 23 Wall Street, I did. The façade, pockmarked by anarchist explosives, was depicted in every school and college text as the symbol of international capitalism. I'd heard the populist farmers and ranchers who were our neighbors in the outback railing against the Wall Street financiers, who, in their minds, were solely responsible for the Great Depression. Their broad Australian voices were in my head as I slipped through the door to escape the heavy snow. I thought, "Why, here's little old Jill Ker from Coorain coming to tell the Morgan Bank it hasn't measured up." The comic disparity between the voices echoing in my head and the role I now played was so great I began to shake with laughter even as I was greeted by one of the discreet but very large security men who welcome every entrant to the bank. To compose my features, I gazed up at the enormous Venetian chandelier that dominates the bank's first floor. My gaze was so intent it amused the security guard, who leaned over, nudged me confidentially, and muttered, "Wanna buy a chandelier, lady?" With that I was summoned to my business, looking much cheerier than the occasion warranted.

The effort to understand endowment management paid off handsomely. Even though I had established a reputation as a fundraiser, Smith's endowment grew just as much through appreciation as through the addition of new capital. There being no senior women money managers in the mid-seventies, we found Smith fathers and husbands who ran successful money management firms to serve as trustees, assess our portfolio strategy, and watch over our own stable of money managers. With their help, we managed not to lose during market corrections the gains we had made in good times. So the $74 million endowment I found was pushing $225 million when I left, and I had developed what was to be a lifelong fascination with financial markets.

If the alumnae relationship was deeply satisfying, and a constant expansion of my perspective on life, Smith students were a joy. I taught classes in history and American studies. I met students in the President's House, sat around the living room, and stopped for morning coffee or afternoon tea. It was a setting that turned intellectual life from a classroom to a conversation, broke the student/teacher hierarchy, and where there were older women students, allowed for children to stop by and play in the garden after school while their mothers finished an afternoon class. I believed a college for women should model an intellectual life that recognized that human beings had a reproductive life; it should not set intellectual effort in opposition to generativity. The afternoon milk and cookies for the children gave me not just their alumnae mothers as lifetime friends, but also another generation of children who thought of themselves as alumni of my classes.

Smith women read the assignments, thought about them, and with encouragement, pushed beyond established categories to arrive at new perspectives on a discipline. It was always fun in a course on feminism to challenge the current ideological verities and watch the results. If women built relationships based exclusively on maternal empathy (as was the current maternalist dogma), did that mean they could only govern a face-to-face community, because they'd be unable to form other sorts of political bonds? And what were we to make of female child abusers? How did their negative maternal feelings fit into female bonding? I wanted my students tough-minded and able to critique their own most seductively comfortable assumptions. Ours was a Socratic mode of discussion, one I've always found perfectly adaptable to looking at the world from a woman's experience. I loved teaching the history honors course on historiography to women already serious about being historians and, unlike my generation, quite certain that there would be a place for them in the scholarly professions. It's endlessly fascinating to read Thucydides, or Hegel and Marx, with a fresh new generation, watch what explanatory strategies seem persuasive for them, and help complicate and enrich the universal historian's task of interpreting a text. Sitting in the bow window of the living room in the President's House, talking about the philosophy of history with half a dozen brilliant and committed students, combined the contemplative and the questing intellectual energy I enjoyed most, and drew me from the onslaught of a thousand administrative decisions to the telos of the place.

I also loved the lively, noisy sense of ownership Smith women displayed about the campus. I liked to listen to the spontaneously raised voices of students chaffing one another, or barracking in the heated rivalry generated by intramural athletic contests. I'd spent many years on coeducational campuses without hearing women's voices raised in unselfconscious ownership of place and event. The noise level at Smith was the sound of women in charge.

There was a campus tradition of student nonsense riots as delightful as it was wacky. Smith's student explosions usually came from the Quad, the part of the campus where almost half the student body lived, in a series of elegant brick buildings that faced one another across a traditional quadrangle. It opened onto Paradise Road, a hundred or so yards from the entrance to the President's House. Most eruptions of youthful energy came at spring examination time, when it was warm enough to race around the campus comfortably, and when tensions had mounted about midterms or finals. The most memorable one for me came on a spring night in 1980, just before midterms.

One resident of the Quad had just earned a substantial check from her grandmother for the laudable achievement of staying on the wagon, and also for not smoking, for a year. In the *ivresse* of the moment, the year's discipline vanished in an euphorically bibulous celebration that spread like contagion through the Quad houses. Soon one side of the Quad eliminated all hope of further study. Every student who possessed a powerful sound system placed the speakers in the open windows and simultaneously turned on the *1812 Overture* at top volume. The opposite side, not to be outclassed, did likewise with "Everybody must get stoned."

I never bothered about the din from the Quad, because it was the Dean of Students' responsibility, and on this, as on many other things relating to students, I was a firm believer in delegation. A life lived on, or close to, university campuses makes one come to enjoy the sound of young people having fun, and to accept a noise level others might find tiresome, so I was drifting off to sleep when the sounds of the evening conveyed unmistakably that the crowd was coming to call. I pulled on slacks and a sweater and made it to the front door just as several hundred barefoot women, scantily clad for the April night, arrived shouting cheery greetings and volunteering to sing Smith songs for me. By the time John joined me, they wanted to be sung to in return, and gave thunderous applause to John's spirited tenor rendition of "When Irish Eyes Are Smiling." Around one-thirty, after much singing, chanting, and speechmaking, I noticed many bare feet turning blue, so I told them they were beginning to look chilly and should go home. Negotiations about the terms for settling down were quickly concluded. Stern comments about overindulgence in alcohol were clearly for the morning. Right now they needed to get inside and get warm. John and I agreed to come and have a nightcap in each of the four main Quad houses if they would go home and go to bed.

It was after two-thirty when we strolled home, having downed the required doses of the dreadfully cheap tequila that was the current student fad. I had a major trustee meeting on this same morning, but it was impossible not to enjoy the instant mass mania of the young on a high. Clearly, the Dean of Students and I hadn't yet succeeded in our alcohol education program, but that was for tomorrow. Needless to say, the winner of the bet who set off the happening grew up to become an exemplary citizen and alumna and a generous donor, with very affectionate memories of her personal moment of folly.

During my decade, Smith added another strong theme to its student culture through the Ada Comstock Scholars Program, an admission program for older women that opened in 1975. Adas were admitted to a regular Smith undergraduate program and received the same financial aid investment as regular-age students. I'd always promised myself that I'd honor my mother's memory someday, somewhere, by making academic institutions take older women seriously as students, instead of seeing them as over-the-hill fee payers without serious intellectual goals. My mother had been widowed at forty-four and would have shone in university-level study, but such things were unheard of in the 1940s. While receiving the superb education she arranged for me, I watched her take jobs beneath her intelligence and try to study on her own. It didn't work, so she slid into depression, suburban loneliness, and the usual palliatives of tranquilizers and brandy. The last half of her life was a sadness I carried close to my heart. I'd vowed to honor her frustrated intellectual dreams by seeing to it that older women students were given serious opportunities, and Smith gave me the chance to fulfill the vow.

In 1975, Smith had already begun to encounter a new generation of older women mobilized by the feminist movement, bent on remaking their lives. Their growing presence meant that Smith's Board and faculty were already prepared to support an admission program with appropriate financial aid for older women students. In 1976, we found in the Charles Stuart Mott Foundation a donor ready to fund a segment of the program focused on the needs of women on welfare, mothers of all ages and types shut out from quality education by having to be at home caring for their children. The new admissions stream for older students was a great academic success, and a valuable supplement to admissions when the pool of traditional-age students temporarily declined in the early 1990s. Decades later, the Adas are an important part of Smith. Though they didn't know it, those wonderful, gutsy older women, determined to remake their lives, helped me to lay my unhappy mother's ghost at least partially to rest, a private need met by a larger and important public purpose.

I'll never forget the mother who came to Northampton the year before we'd raised money for supporting the needs of welfare women with children. She and her two children began the academic year homeless, because no one would rent to her. She was literally spending her days in Seelye Hall attending philosophy classes, and going back to her car to study beside her two children, shining a flashlight on her assigned reading from Plato and Aristotle. I learned about her because she brought her children to the annual student reception, and I asked them where they were in school. The answer introduced me to another world. "We can't go to school. We have no address. Mom's on welfare, and no one will rent to her."

We soon found them housing, and through her and the other welfare mothers who came to Smith, we learned ways to thwart the welfare bureaucracy. Because every cent we gave them directly was deducted from their welfare payments, an academically talented woman could only get an education at the expense of her children's health and diet. In a small town, we quickly learned to pay the pharmacy and the food market directly, so that no formal grant reduced a woman's welfare check and yet needed food and medical supplies were available.

Each year at Commencement, I was close to tears when it came to handing out the diplomas to the graduating Adas, especially the welfare mothers, some of whom graduated summa cum laude. Their start in life had overwhelmed them with psychological or economic burdens, but a modest capital investment and real psychological support had allowed hidden talents to flourish. This was education working as nineteenth-century educational idealists believed it should. Watching the transformation from woman-on-the-economic-margins to woman-in-charge-of-her-life made the frustrations of a president's job sink into total insignificance. The sight of the triumphant face and confident step up to the platform to receive the degree was always juxtaposed in my mind with the picture of the hesitant, worried person who'd arrived as a first-year Ada. There is no satisfaction greater than witnessing such a transformation.

I'd come to Smith determined that the woman who joyfully clutched that diploma at graduation would have the best resources Smith could muster to support her next phase of life. Women had had access to higher education in North America for more than a century, yet even in 1975 there was no smooth articulation between women graduates and the world of work. I soon realized that my personal crusade to see that Smith women got good career counseling could differentiate Smith from its competitors. Smith in the fifties and sixties, like all women's colleges, and society generally, had been ambivalent about the place of paid work in women's lives. I knew we'd bypass the competition if Smith became known as the place where women got the best counseling about work, and the most aggressive and well-networked career services to help them test out possible career paths.

I knew we could be way ahead of coeducational competitors on this score, because coeducational schools all operated on an assimilation model that fitted women into what already existed for men. That ignored the double messages women received about self and family, and glossed over the differences in development between women and men in early adulthood. When we began recruiting the staff and developing the programs that helped students deal with the fact that, unlike men, women have to develop both a professional self and a generative self during the transition from adolescence to young adulthood, faculty members were critical and trustees were worried by what was called "Jill's vocationalism." But I wasn't planning on just slotting Smith graduates into the often dead-end going jobs for women liberal arts graduates. I wanted them to graduate having thought seriously about the juxtaposition of work and generativity in their lives, taking with them some realistic sense of what it might mean to work in different types of organizations, industries, professions, creative callings.

So Smith's Vocational Office became Smith's Career Development Office, with enlarged facilities and staff, and I made a major investment in a service usually scorned by liberal arts faculties. But unlike my male predecessors, and faculty critics, I knew from my own life how intense an existential crisis settling the place of work and family in a woman's life could be. The world around one talked with a forked tongue, on the one hand urging academic achievement and on the other pointing out that a woman's happiness lay in suppressing the drive for achievement in the interests of a "happy" marriage. It was great to have the feminist movement of the 1970s persuading women that serious work was an important aspect of human creativity from which women had been shut out. But there was still the question of how such work was to be found, and how one filled the page that was blank in most women's life scripts about how work was to be meshed with family.

A woman president could talk honestly about filling that blank page. My male predecessors had made the student Baccalaureate service an occasion for avuncular advice, but I talked with as much humor and wisdom as I could muster about the double roles of women and the ways I thought they were best managed. I still meet women in just about every American city who stop me on the street and say, "I've never forgotten the Baccalaureate service, and I've followed most of your advice. I never took the double binds personally, because Smith gave me a sense of women's history and where I stood in it. And when I've had a big assignment at work and the house is a mess, I remember that you taught us dust has no moral significance, and I'm not a failed woman if the kids are sick, my husband's cross, and the laundry is lost."

Hiring talented professionals and fostering research on women and work, especially on the transition from college, was an investment that paid off. In the late eighties and early nineties, years of substantial unemployment for college graduates, Smith's senior classes knew how to look for the right job and how to function in different work settings. And when the trough in the number of high school graduates entering college heated up admissions competition in the early nineties, counseling and employment networks helped to attract potential students.

As I sent the new alumnae out the door, I worried about the gap between women's earnings and men's of the same level of education (58 cents on the dollar in the 1970s). Clearly, while that ratio remained, the return on a woman's education would be vastly less than that of her male peers. I knew we couldn't close the gap by persuading society to pay teaching and nursing better. That's not how labor markets work. The gap would only narrow if women entered the high-earning professions and the business world. I thought entry into the high-earning professions would take care of itself as quotas limiting women's enrollment in the best professional schools were made unlawful. But moving women beyond the secretarial and clerical ghettos of the modern corporation was a tougher problem. We needed to map out a path that made it possible for young women to join the executive training ranks of the corporation just as men from elite colleges and universities did.

Creating the map turned out to be simpler than I'd thought. With the help and coaching of the knowledgeable and well-connected alumna leading Smith's corporate fundraising, I began calling on CEOs of Fortune 500 companies to ask why they didn't recruit on the Smith campus. Their recruiters stopped at Amherst en route to Dartmouth and Williams, but went right by Smith in Northampton, and Mount Holyoke next door in South Hadley. Once I'd secured a promise to correct the oversight, I could ask why the list of Company X's contributions to higher education didn't include gifts to women's colleges, which offered a significant pool of talent to be tapped—an important pool in an era of affirmative action. Most CEOs had never thought of women's colleges in that light, even though usually their wives had attended one.

That discussion led to a longer conversation about the kinds of preparation Company X sought in recruiting into its executive ranks. It was a long conversation, because most CEOs had strong opinions about higher education and enjoyed the chance to express them to an attentive listener. Invariably, broad general education was the most desired quality, together with skills in language and foreign cultures, which were needed in international business. Just as my host was expressing regret that no one studied languages anymore, I could point out that women had never abandoned language studies, and a high proportion of Smith's graduates had studied in foreign universities, not only in Europe but in Japan and China as well. If I was visiting a technology-based company, I could list the little-known but important statistics about the high percentage of women trained in science at women's colleges who persisted in full-time scientific careers. I usually left not only with Company X's promise to recruit at Smith and other women's colleges, but also with some unrestricted funds in hand, and a contact person to whom I could send Smith's career counseling staff to discuss developing summer internships.

To most faculty colleagues and some trustees, the time investment on this program didn't make sense. But they forgot that I hadn't gone to school with the leaders of American business. I didn't belong to their clubs, and was not a golfer, so I wasn't likely to meet them at their popular recreation. Some such effort was necessary. In any event, the stratagem worked. Smith moved to the top ranks of liberal arts colleges in corporate support, and decades before experiential learning was the fashion, the career counselors used the growing supply of internships to very good effect. The result was a growing young alumnae group of corporate executives, and the beginnings of a higher earnings profile for Smith classes. It would be decades before we'd know if this was sustained through their lifetime, but at least the path had been blazed and the map of the best routes to follow was getting more and more detailed every day. All these changes were gratifying steps toward redefining Smith as an institution that was committed to meeting the educational needs of all women—not just eighteen-to-twenty-two-year olds, and not just affluent, well-prepared students—in ways that recognized the realities of women's lives in the late twentieth century.

But there were components of the job that never seemed to change, and one of those was the tiresome anxieties some alumnae, the media, and even some trustees constantly expressed over the sexual life of Smith undergraduates. When I came to Smith in 1975, it was young women's too-active heterosexual life that bothered people. By the early 1980s, the obsession was with women's homoerotic life. It seemed as if never a day went by that someone didn't ask me what I was doing about some aspect of young women's sexuality. The questioners always acted as though I were some supermother figure who could chivy her girls into being "good." I could feel my body tense and my voice become clipped with anger at the unspoken assumption that women in their twenties were still "girls" whose erotic life should be owned and controlled by someone else. Everyone smiled tolerantly about young men's sexual adventures in their college years, and thought men entitled to adventure and experiment. But not young women. People still made the easy assumption that society was entitled to control young women's sexuality. It made me angry that the questioners wanted only to know about what was happening to those vaginas, and seemed to have no interest in the intellectual life and academic mission that brought young women to Smith.

Another constant was the worry of older faculty, some alumnae from the 1950s and '60s, and some alumnae trustees that all these new programs might be making Smith too "feminist." This, of course, was a word no one could define precisely. Smith was an institution founded on nineteenth-century feminist principles, and over its first century of life the feminist parts of its mission were constantly redefined in line with contemporary understanding of women's social and political roles. I was troubling people by the pace at which I was moving to link women's education to new professions and careers. So it was an uphill battle to get people to agree to a dual-degree program in engineering, offered in partnership with the University of Massachusetts School of Engineering, but there was no problem at all about a new graduate program in dance. Worry though they might, however, trustees and alumnae leaders showed a touching willingness to back my program of change, even though the notion of full-time professional careers for young mothers was one that worried an older generation a lot. I was pushing hard because I thought that only real clarity of vision about the educational needs of women in the 1990s and beyond would give Smith a clear competitive edge—and I was grateful for the Board's solid support.

Another constant of the job was the total lack of disposable time. Presidents' offices in private colleges are always understaffed, because the demands of the job are hard to convey to all the constituencies whose experience touches only one part of the job. It's a life of hectic entertaining to keep in touch with trustees, faculty, alumni, student groups, donors, and political allies. We once kept count at 8 Paradise Road and found that in a year I offered food and hospitality to about five thousand people. So the staff at the house mattered every bit as much as the office. To arrive home at 8 Paradise Road, where the staff was bustling with preparations for a Board dinner of eighty, was always to be reminded that a woman president is also her own hostess, and she's judged not only for her management expertise but also for the style and ambience of her household. Mine was cheerful and relaxed because of Maxine Mason, a cook of genius and a personality on campus. An African-American woman of great physical and spiritual beauty, she could be found on weekends or afternoons when there wasn't a formal function surrounded by students who'd come for advice or to escape homesickness or exam panic, aided by Max's famous cakes and cookies. She never failed them or me. Her lieutenant and my other great source of calm was Michael Yanginski, the house custodian and my driver, who always got me wherever I had to go exactly on time despite snow, ice, and hurricanes. The first sign of coming home from a trip was always walking out on the arrivals level at the airport to see Michael waiting, clutching the bag of papers sent from the office for me to work on in the car on the way home. It was reassuring to have such an unflappable team in the house, because I was never quite sure who'd be at breakfast, why they were there, or how long they were staying. Once I came back from my early morning swim to find John at breakfast cheerfully discussing the details of the D Day landings in Normandy with William Westmoreland. The general was visiting to publicize his new book of memoirs, but no one had remembered to tell me. I didn't really need to know such details, because Max, Michael, and Connie Coggswell, who took care of the upstairs, coped so well with running what often seemed like a small private hotel. It was always interesting, but occasionally wearing.

But when the events were over and the guests had departed, there were always four or five hours of dictation every night, in those pre-email days, to keep up with the mountain of correspondence, fundraising proposals, legislative briefings, committee reports, and all the rest, which arrived on my desk every day. Even though people may take several weeks to answer a letter themselves, everyone complains about the turnaround time for correspondence in the President's Office. One can't miss responding quickly to the major donor, to the chairman of a Board committee, to the student government, the faculty council, a potentially hostile reporter. One can't let sloppy proposals go to foundations. Pretty soon one begins to see oneself as a cluster of resources limited only by physical stamina, to be deployed as effectively as possible across the gamut of all these contending needs. Looking at oneself in this fashion might be seen as a form of alienation, since it's a form of surrendering the self to an institution. And that can often lead to submerging personal identity in an institution with demands that can never be totally met.

Many presidents fall into that trap. The total spectrum of creative things one can do on the job is very seductive. Is one an architect manqué? There are always buildings to be built and renovated. I started my career as a builder of athletic facilities at the University of Toronto and finished my decade at Smith by building a field house and Olympic-size track-and-field facilities that allowed the athletic program to flourish. In the process, I mastered intricate details about the discus and shot put, and developed strong views on the surfacing of tracks. It was a delight for someone definitely a jock at heart. A frustrated landscape designer? There was an entire building and grounds and horticulture staff to deploy. To walk around a beautiful rural campus turning one's eye to how this vista or that slope might be enhanced or pulled into the overall design was total gratification. Most of us don't have a public landscape to work with on a scale like that of the eighteenth-century English and French aristocracy. A lover of early music? There was a nascent program to nurture its performance along. Stagestruck? There was the Theater Department busy developing its program in a new theater. I liked watching the program in stage fighting introduced early in my time at Smith. It seemed like a discipline I had much to learn from.

I'd always been too clumsy to dance. But I loved ballet and relished the chance to plan and develop the most comprehensive dance program to be found outside a school of performing arts. Everything left out of one's education, or out of one's skills and talents, can be realized in surrogate form as the head of an academic institution. It can be so endlessly fascinating that one forgets other ways of living.

But as a counter to such protean pleasures, there is also the presidential role as magistrate: the place of last resort for students who have breached college rules, for faculty denied reappointment or tenure, and staff who have been terminated. The process that leads up to denial of faculty tenure or expulsion of a student is long, contentious, and extremely painful. A college is a face-to-face community, so virtually everyone takes sides. I learned to restrain a natural tendency to be open and warm toward the wounded young scholar, or the heartbroken student, because the mere fact of a sympathetic hearing exacerbated the outrage if my later decision was negative.

It was impossible to study the cases that came before me without asking myself subversive questions about the issues. I thought the tenure process often corrupt, because senior faculty could always muster specious reasons why X's work was substandard. It made me wonder whether faculty wouldn't be better off trading higher compensation and reasonable termination arrangements for a process that, once contested, damaged the victim seemingly irreparably. Departments overruled could see to it that the victim perished slowly through ostracism. Scholars whose work was truly on the margin between good and not-so-good never regained their confidence. I thought there were sufficient legal protections for free speech and the expression of contentious scholarly opinions in the late twentieth century, and that the tenure system was no longer necessary to protect academic freedom. Instead it simply fostered a pernicious tyranny of the old over the young. I tried to imagine what the separation might be like for the younger faculty denied tenure if they had not been so poor they were in hock to the institution for the second mortgage on their house and had had so little discretionary income that they hadn't been able to save for the inevitable emergencies in life. I found being the judge in these cases deeply disillusioning.

Students who broke the rules presented even more troubling issues. Cases of cheating were the worst, because of the slice of family life revealed as one tried to assess the motivation for the offense, and whether the offender was a habitual cheater, or someone who'd cracked under extraordinary stress and might learn not to appropriate others' work as her own in the future. One saw driven parents projecting impossible aspirations on cowed children, and became painfully aware of the stalled moral and emotional growth of the child who has never been allowed her own motivations. Young people who'd never entertained a single motive of their own lived in a world of panic and moral rootlessness it was chilling to behold. Although the formal rules left few options, I couldn't help trying to imagine an educational system that could really help such victims. What might be made of people who were good copiers? The system had no place for them, but theirs would be admirable talents in, say, Japan, where accurate imitation was valued. It gave me a heavy heart to tell them and their invincibly insensitive parents that the offender must leave. What life ahead held for them wasn't pleasant to contemplate.

Like every presidential colleague I knew, I often pondered the mores of the faculty whose task it was to instill the ideal of the golden mean in their students. In most cases, there was a wildly comical gap between the ideal espoused and the way many people behaved outside the classroom. Faculty meetings and academic processions always set me pondering the mystery of how people behave in relation to what they teach. There was always a small group whose liberal ideals permeated every aspect of their lives. I could not have lived without them. They were the glue that kept the institution together.

There were others who took their academic calling as a license for eccentricity, so that on down days one might see one's institution more as like a leaky ship of fools, or a particularly shady set of pilgrims bound for Canterbury, than as an embodiment of the Platonic ideals by which my small group of esteemed faculty lived. I had a great admiration for Erasmus, especially for his satirical *In Praise of Folly*, and thought a comic vision essential for my job. In faculty meetings, I always had plenty of material to work on. There was the near tragedy turned comedy of the mercurial modern language instructor who, in a fit of drug-induced depression, attempted suicide by shooting himself in the head with a spearfishing gun and mercifully survived to wander around the campus in search of help, looking like someone from *William Tell*. There were the dangerously unfit people with pendulous stomachs who staggered to their feet at faculty meetings to denounce athletics as a waste of money. The followers of F. R. Leavis, who scorned to speak to literary scholars of other persuasions. The tone-deaf, who thought music unintellectual. Those whose very being proclaimed their lack of aesthetic sense, who could see no value in studio art.

Yet present any of these people with a student and a blackboard and they were transformed into models of Socratic instruction. By the end of my first few years at Smith, I could see that although in all other respects we were a great parade of eccentrics, the faculty was united in instilling a love of learning in the young. And when I looked at myself trailing along at the end of the procession, I was amused at the naiveté that kept me, in midlife, expecting that there was a simple and unambiguous relationship between knowledge and conduct. I still had a lot to learn on the job. And doubtless someday I'd learn from some helpful commentator just how my behavior contradicted the lofty historical ideals I loved to teach.

5

SCHOLARS WITH PINES

❀ FROM THE DAY I ARRIVED in Northampton, I was on guard against the presidential trap of merging self and institution so completely that there seemed no life outside the role. I'd had trouble with boundaries earlier in life and wasn't about to repeat the predicament. My childhood and youth had been times of struggle to connect inner and outer self. The external world of repeated family tragedies was too hard to risk really inhabiting, and my private view of the story unfolding in the adult world around me was too dark to talk about. So that left me a blank page in public, something on which kindly family, well-meaning schools, generous friends, professional educators could all project a persona.

Until the moment of rebellion arrived in my early twenties, when I rejected all the well-intentioned prescriptions for my life and left Australia in search of a place where I could investigate the elusive self I scarcely knew. Graduate school, distance from Australia, and family allowed me to complete the archetypal coming-of-age process. I felt I owned who I was, and that the private me was no stranger to her public self-presentation. It was like coming into a port that was a real safe haven when I found the mate who agreed enthusiastically with my self-definition and didn't seem to want to improve on it.

Doing the conventional things—marrying, beginning a scholarly career—gave me a false sense of security, as though the task of relating inner and outer self had been definitively completed. As a young married woman in my thirties, I expected that there weren't going to be too many more iterations of the quest for self-definition. But, of course, I was wrong. I wasn't quite forty when I arrived at Smith and ran instantly into one of the major challenges of adulthood. That challenge is to protect and sustain the inner self we've labored so hard to release while fully entering into the roles we have to play as adults with major symbolic, professional, and personal responsibilities. The coming-of-age story doesn't deal with what we have to do to sustain the inner self against all the structures of society—family, professions, voluntary institutions, political movements, competing vocations—all of which demand conformity to their ideal types.

One of the most seductive attractions of the romantic view of life is the notion that there exists somewhere the perfect partner who resonates emotionally to every note of one's own inner music. And that there is one vocation we are destined to take up in which we will find nothing out of key and experience no disharmonies between our working and private self. But the reality is otherwise. Most people are a cluster of talents that could potentially be applied in myriad different ways. The young need career counseling for just this reason. And the rate of divorce tells us that the uniquely preordained soul mate is hard to find. So the challenge in adulthood is to sustain that inner self while entering passionately into a complicated set of relationships, any one of which may constrain who we are. The alternative is to stand back from life or to choose the "safe" commitments that don't demand too much. I was born a risk taker. Safety was never attractive. So when it came to marriage, I brushed aside all well-meant counsels of caution and married someone a generation older than me.

It was a great cast of the dice. The woman who marries a much older man can become a target of the Pygmalion syndrome. But I didn't. I had the good sense to marry a teacher of genius when I still had a lot to learn about self and work. Some teachers of genius have massive egos and insist on cramming their students into a replica of themselves. There are others who can see intuitively the lineaments of the inner person and figure out what's necessary to bring them into full, three-dimensional embodiment. The Greeks called the culmination of such a process *areté*, and John Conway understood his mission in life to be to bring those he taught and loved to such a point. It was a mission he followed generously with people of all ages and levels of talent, and nowhere more devotedly than with a wife eighteen years his junior. But of necessity, the span of the generation that stood between us meant that I was in a hurry to catch up, rushing past stages in personal development I had to complete later.

We both believed in theory that privacy was a bourgeois ideal, a self-indulgent aspect of commercial values, to be contrasted negatively with the more admirable ideal of public service. So for John our marriage wasn't stressed by my pattern of life as a college president—a pattern that involved constant entertainment, frequent long absences, and a schedule of appointments that kept me, when home, busy from eight in the morning until ten-thirty at night. But I was stressed. Not by all the public commitments but by the lack of solitude. A solitary childhood and adolescence and a reflective temperament meant that I just had to be alone sometimes to retain my sanity. And a life of hard work on the family sheep station made me crave hard physical labor as an antidote to the overly intellectual life. I might have become an urban intellectual, but I didn't feel like one. I thought the Benedictine rule of work, prayer, and meditation saner than any other rule for life I knew, and I began to lose my zest for life if I couldn't find some approximation of it.

So within months of arriving in Northampton we began looking for a house in the hill towns overlooking the Connecticut Valley. It had to be quiet, extremely simple, and too small to accommodate too many overnight guests. Its kitchen had to be the right size for a woman who loves to cook and talk to the assembled company at the same time. And it had to have enough land to make a serious garden. It had to be close enough so that we could reach it quickly on weekends and so that I could commute from it to the office for part of the summer.

When we found it, it was just a few miles from our surrogate parents, Archie and Ada MacLeish, in the town of Conway, just eighteen miles from Northampton but psychologically very distant. It was captivating to live in a town that bore John's family name, but even more captivating was the house. It had been perfectly sited, sitting on bedrock with a steep drop down to the Mill River, which was just a glint of light through the woods in winter but a steady sound in the summer. It overlooked a north-facing slope and a south-facing slope, and it perched at the top of so many different levels of land zig-zagging down to the river that from a distance it seemed to be riding on its promontory like some tiny Italian hill town.

It was built of pine, glass, and grey granite from a nearby quarry, and oriented east and west so that its walls of glass and stone floors captured solar energy in winter when the leaves were down. It was shaded in summer, when the woods were in full leaf, and cooled by the bedrock on which it sat. Its designers and owners had loved the simple life in the woods, so the giant trees from the surrounding old-growth forest came right up to the house on three sides of a building that had its back firmly turned to the road.

We liked the plain pine walls and stone floors, the openness to the woods, but we were gardeners, and immediately set about clearing space for a garden and opening up a vista to the distant hills. The vista was framed by two enormous white pines standing above exposed grey ledge ringed with moss. It all looked so quiet and reflective that it could have been a Japanese or Chinese scroll painting, complete with a mandarin figure contemplating nature. Here, just thirty minutes away from Smith, I found a North American variant of the quiet and solitude of my Australian plains.

Our life in Conway took place on snatched fragments of weekends, holidays, and summers. It revolved around creating a garden, hiking to enjoy the striking beauty of the natural landscape, poetry, which we read aloud to one another almost every evening we were alone, and music.

But the garden came first. To create it we had to clear selected spots of light among the pines, oaks, elms, and maples that towered more than a hundred feet above the forest floor, and then clear the understory of saplings and brush, to replant it with smaller shrubs and trees. We were both passionate landscape designers, so that every walk around the twelve acres we owned involved sudden stops to view the light, choices about developing this or that vista, lengthy reflections on which should be the focal point in a landscape naturally irregular, craggy, and strong in primal shapes.

Since John had lost his right hand and lower arm in a war injury, he was restricted to working on pulling weeds, or wielding clippers on small saplings, but I set to work with saw and hatchet to tackle larger trees, swinging joyfully at the more recalcitrant, thinking cheerfully of them as faculty enemies to be vanquished. After a year of work, we were ready to plant the rhododendrons, laurels, crab apples, and dogwoods that domesticated the landscape, working on weekends with two gardeners moonlighting from the Smith gardens who became our partners, as engrossed as we in the emerging design.

I'd never gardened in a climate where spring bulbs flourished, but John had. He chose as his major design task the selection and planting of thousands of bulbs, so that early to late spring became a lyrical crescendo of gold, white, blue, and scarlet. I worked on planting ground covers, because all the grades were too steep for lawns, and we wanted to be gardeners who didn't pollute the river below with fertilizers and weed killers. Mine was a design problem in shades of green, and a planting task for someone with a strong back and supple knees. So for most of our three earliest summers there, when I wasn't swinging an ax I was on my knees planting ground covers. Everything grew well in the woodsy, acidic soil, so I could make living tapestries of different shades of green, choosing textures to reflect or contain light and shapes to accentuate or cloak a contour of land.

It took four years to decide where to put the swimming pool so that it would not make the landscape suburban. It was tucked away on a level above the house, its shape blasted from the bedrock. A swimming pool required a pond to fill it from, so we used the blasted rock to support a dam built around a spring forty feet below the house. Once there was water and reflected sky from the pond on one side of the house, it clearly required balancing by a fountain and the sound of water on the other—my project for a wall fountain that recalled every courtyard I loved in Rome.

Neither one was critical of even the most grandiose landscaping plans of the other. We were happy to be just like the eighteenth-century English landed gentry—close to insolvency because of the grandeur of our garden designs.

After a decade, we found a stonemason of extraordinary talent who shaped and bounded the landscape with dry stone walls and paved paths that were works of art. When planting and drawing out the shape of the earth seemed close to accomplishment, our desires turned to outdoor sculpture to capture the spirit of the place, not with eighteenth-century fauns and nymphs but with spare modern bronze and granite. We argued unceasingly but amiably. Where to plant this bush? What variety of holly should go here? How should this young witch hazel be pruned? Emerging around us as the years passed was a canvas with details that grew clearer every year. The garden was an endless delight.

It was also the pivot on which a great friendship turned. In my first year at Smith, Kathy Pitney, an alumna with a justly earned reputation as a fundraiser for the Republican Party, and for education and the arts, had snatched time away from nursing her husband back to health after a major heart attack to drive up from New Jersey regularly to spend the day advising me about how best to build support for Smith. She was such an expert that although I'd worry about her driving back to be near her husband after a long day of meetings, I came to rely on her a lot. On our first visit to Pitney Farm, in Mendham, New Jersey, we found her presiding over a great garden, and an eighteenth-century farmhouse of classic beauty. Duncan Pitney—a painter, musician, and former World War II bomber pilot—was an equally avid landscape designer and painter. So began a pattern of spring vacations taken together to explore great gardens, summer landscape and outdoor sculpture expeditions, and long conversations about how to build our rock-laden Massachusetts garden. The pattern became set for a lifetime.

In Conway, gardening was for mornings and early afternoons. By three o'clock, unless we had sedentary guests, we were studying geological survey maps to plan the hike that would bring us through some new terrain, provide a promising outlook on the Connecticut River Valley or a distant view of mountains in New Hampshire and Vermont. Mostly, the two of us walked alone—occasionally in companionable silence but usually in the kind of long, leisurely conversation that allows for slow circling about all aspects of a subject. Sometimes the hills and valleys and streams were backdrops for refighting the battles of the Second World War. Sometimes they overlooked extended discussions of music, composers, philosophy, history, travel, literary criticism, art. It was the conversation idealized in Greek dialogues, the fundamental grounding of a spiritual and moral as well as physical relationship. We were never bored with one another because we were temperamental opposites: John the romantic, Dionysian temperament, I the Apollonian seeker of balance and symmetry. So no subject was ever finished, though eventually our aching legs and feet would prompt us to turn homeward.

Our country retreat was a wonderful antidote to a fast-paced life full of waiting cars, helicopters, split-second schedules, endless public speaking, total concentration on the major donor—everything so carefully orchestrated there was scarcely the chance to put a foot in a puddle. It was all well worth doing, but to balance it I needed to come wearily home from a chilly walk, almost too tired to speak, prepare a simple meal, and then sit before the fire with John as we read our favorite poetry aloud together. We often shared the walks and the poetry with Jack Bate, one of John's oldest Harvard friends and a literary scholar of encyclopedic learning. He lived for poetry, and his voice reading it carried the immediacy of hearing it for the first time.

And it was there that I could escape from my role and enjoy the small group of faculty friends who were able to separate me as a person from the office I was discharging. So the intensely personal elements of life were snatched here, around the edges of things, in the interstices of the academic year. There were only two couples at Smith in whom I confided about John's manic-depressive illness. Dick Unsworth, the College chaplain, his wife, Joy, and their family of beautiful children became part of our extended family. Ours was an ecumenical friendship based on common approaches to religious experience. We shared the Chapel and its mission, all the liturgical occasions embedded in the academic year. We also shared Dick's love of music and the college celebrations where he appeared not in clerical garb but as player of a mean bass fiddle.

Connie and Frank Ellis, my other confidants, were our nearest neighbors in Northampton, living in the pretty red frame house that stood just across the path past 8 Paradise Road, opposite our front door. We had literary and artistic tastes in common. Frank was an advertising man turned scholar of English literature of the Augustan age. Connie, once a doctrinaire member of the Communist Party during her passionate youth at Vassar, was a connoisseur of the decorative arts and a guiding presence at the Smith Museum of Art. Most of all, we loved conversation, good food, and gardens. We dined together often, shared the same wedding anniversary, and always celebrated it jointly as the campus settled into the quiet before Christmas. Sometimes, because of the anniversary nature of John's manic spells, it would be a celebration of three rather than four. The great blessing of the friendship was that although Frank was often on opposing sides of many of my faculty battles, we went for an entire decade never once referring to them.

Joyce Berkman, John's colleague in history at the University of Massachusetts, and her husband, Len, a playwright in Smith's Theater Department, gave us the extra pleasure of knowing their young children. We shared history, music, theater, and like political views, and managed a friendship focused on new playwrights, new historical insights, contemporary art, and literature, our conversations utterly devoid of current academic gossip.

Later, there were wonderful young people to share our Conway walks, nieces and nephews in school or college nearby—the surrogate children all childless couples need. With them, the conversations expanded from the viewpoint and experiences of a fresh generation, and the verse repertory was enlarged by a new set of tastes. The extended family circle gave a pattern to the year, shaped by Easter, Thanksgiving, Christmas, and spring and autumn school breaks. So the house and its surrounding garden became a focal point in a sustaining network that nourished a private self, which simply had no space in my daily working round.

To me, life in Conway meant the simplicity and quiet that I needed to retain from my childhood. I'd grown up closer to nature than most lives ever encompass, herding sheep and cattle across the vast, empty plains of inland Australia. That had given me a deeply religious sense of the creation. I needed to get back to it as a psychological anchor, or I felt adrift, unmoored, rudderless at the confluence of too many currents. I needed the solitude to draw the curtain on all the public roles I played—to set the performance temporarily to one side and meditate a little on what it was all about.

Music was the nonverbal language that helped me do that best. It went right by the brain's rationalizations to the core of one's feelings, so they could be rearranged in the context of harmony and dissonance. John loved great crashing romantic symphonies and concerti. I liked baroque music and the more meditative mood of the string quartet. Often, when alone in Conway, I'd bring along a biography of a favorite composer, borrow all the major works from the Smith Music Library, and play them in the sequence they'd been composed, teaching myself how to listen to music in the process.

Although our life in Conway was idyllic, I needed all the means I could muster to cope with the events that threatened to undermine it. John's manic-depressive illness didn't stabilize with advancing age, as we'd hoped. It grew more acute and took the familiar form of anniversary events. We could be certain that mania would strike somewhere in the first week of June, and somewhere in the week before Christmas. We became familiar with the road to the private psychiatric hospital I took him to at the first warning signs. There was no question that each new incident was more shattering, more undermining to his confidence, than the last, and that the medication program got heavier and heavier, clouding the elegant mind that was our joy. Lithium was the price we had to pay for relative stability, a price that had to be accepted, even though he hated taking a drug that affected his mental acuity. The combination of medications and mood swings meant that he found it harder and harder to concentrate, so that the closing years of his academic career were entirely devoted to teaching, because research and writing eluded him.

That loss was put in perspective in the early 1980s, when what proved to be an unidentifiable disease of the nerve endings struck him, manifesting in its onset all the symptoms of Lou Gehrig's disease. When we were told that he must put his affairs in order and expect death sometime in the next twenty-four months, we entered a bizarre world of unimagined stress. Month by month he lost mobility, every effort to move around accompanied by heavy falls, from which he could not pick himself up. His voice changed, his face became an expressionless mask, he began to have difficulty swallowing. For me it was like watching an execution in slow motion.

Then, miraculously and inexplicably, he began, very slowly, to recover. The disease was not Lou Gehrig's disease but an unknown virus. It was a brush with mortality that changed my perspective on life, reformulated my ambitions, placed career aspirations in a different context. I'd pay my dues to society, but what I wanted was to live every precious minute that remained with this man. When we expected his death, it had been anguishing to be away on long trips, and exhausting to carry out the formal schedule of meetings, entertainment, public speaking. I was the product of a childhood of losses—and now I lived braced for the most crippling loss of all. Even when the damaged nerve endings healed or grew new connections and his mobility inched back almost imperceptibly, I never lost the fear, and never looked at life the same way again.

When I was alone in the house in Conway because John was in the hospital recovering from a manic spell, I would sit listening to a late

Beethoven quartet, watching the dusk fall and the light become luminous, just before dark. I could sit there, holding all the pains and joys together in one moment, in no sense in a happy state of being, but able to accept life's tragedies. I was now well beyond childish rebellion, truly a much older woman, for whom inner and outer self could come together, because I was no longer in panic-stricken retreat from life's grievous blows.

6

AFTER THE LEAVES
ARE DOWN

✥ By my late forties, I'd learned my job and ought to
have been settling down to enjoy its satisfactions. But I had,
instead, a double experience of life's seasons. As if by virtue of my
roots in both northern and southern hemispheres I could experience
high summer and autumn at the same time. The experience of life
simultaneously in two hemispheres meant an inner life with many
circlings back and forth between happiness and the awareness of
tragedy. There was, beside the sunlight at Smith, John's crippling
and apparently irreversible illness.

My mother's death at seventy-nine had removed all illusions that
I could ever make peace with her—a final sorrow, an ending with no
redemption. Shortly after her death, I had another shaping encounter with mortality. I became guardian and caregiver to my nineteen-
year-old Australian niece, an adopted daughter of my brother. A
surrogate for the longed-for daughter, she was a brilliant student
whom it was a delight to introduce to Smith. She died slowly and
anguishingly of leukemia during her sophomore year. She had fought
very hard for life, and I found her loss almost beyond bearing. The
disjunction between private and public experience was a persistent

puzzle. I was living simultaneously in the full summer of a mature career and in the steely-grey phase of late autumn, when one is haunted by last things. My face was indubitably toward the rewards of midlife, but at the edges of my consciousness I could see the shadows lengthening.

The bright side of life was the sense of fruition in my work at Smith. I had a fine team of administrators to manage the operations. The financial indicators in the annual operating budget were all pointing in the right direction and I was free to do what I most enjoyed, to plan and build for the future. My focus was now the next decade, for which I was intent on harnessing whatever fickle gods presided over higher education to help us prepare for the strenuous and testing future.

The strenuosity came from intensifying competition in the 1980s for able students. The pool of high school graduates from which the thirty most selective American universities and colleges drew their students was in decline and would shrink to its lowest point in the early 1990s, to remain there until mid-decade. It was not a market contraction that could be negotiated just by tightening the belt and doing the same with less. It was a time to invest for competitive advantage, and to build resources to ride out some potentially lean years.

I knew that we had the decade of the eighties to create the endowment base and the crisply defined identity that would enable us to hold our place competitively. The problem was to mobilize the institution to share the urgency I felt and to work with me on my vision of the kind of women's institution that would be a winner with the students of the nineties and beyond.

When I sat late at night in the President's Office, surrounded by the shades of my six predecessors, it amused me to think that unlike those six Oxbridge or Ivy products, I was a latter-day Christine de

Pizan (1365–c. 1429), intent on building my community for learned women not brick by brick but chip by chip, so that women could be literate in the wired world that I knew, from years on IBM's World Trade Board, would soon be upon us. Christine de Pizan had written learned treatises on military strategy for her fifteenth-century French court. I was intent on seeing how Smith's students would take charge of the new transforming technologies of information processing.

There were many disciplines we needed to introduce to produce the educated woman of the nineties. She needed the same knowledge as her male peers plus the capacity for decisive action that comes with running one's own world. The fields of knowledge I thought most important were computer science and the study of artificial intelligence, linguistics with the associated field of semiotics (both of which intersected with philosophy), psychology, mathematics, literary studies, neuropsychology, ever-expanding components of molecular biology, the burgeoning specialties in women's studies, African-American studies, and the languages that were the base for the serious study of Asian cultures. Most fell within the old medieval categories of philosophy, language, and mathematics, but the new languages and area studies, once graduate specialties, were now important components of a good general education.

In the early eighties, I was working ahead of the culture wars that erupted over postmodern thought and the abandonment of the centrality of Western European culture. Had I been able to read the future, I would have unhesitatingly made exactly the same choices to expand the curriculum beyond a Western core, knowing what cultural conservatives conveniently forget, the babel of cultures out of which emerged what we think of as a coherent modern European worldview. If a mingling of Arab science and Central Asian invasions contributed to the medieval synthesis of ideas and customs, better knowledge of the great achievements of non-Western cultures, a necessity for a world transformed by communications, was no cultural threat but a stimulus for creativity.

In 1980, we were just ahead of the rising expectations of women high school students whose experience had been changed by Title IX. Contrary to the received faculty view of college sports, student athletes were often the highest academic performers, just the women we wanted to attract. Coeducational schools were laggards in giving women full equality in athletic facilities and their use, and coaching was as yet an art drawn from men's athletics. So we needed to reconfigure our athletic programs to promote serious competition, build unrivaled athletic facilities, and begin to train first-rate coaches in our graduate physical education program.

Such an investment was anathema to most of the academic old guard, with its tired stereotypes about jocks. I neutralized opposition by inviting one of the faculty's most noted academic conservatives to become the first director of a new Athletic Department. He'd been a professional baseball player for some years before beginning graduate study, and was in his seventh heaven building the new program, a task he carried out with efficiency and touching loyalty. Once launched on this road, I had a strong ally in preaching the need to give women the experience of the toughest competition they could encounter, and of the qualities of leadership built by participation in team sports. Tribal loyalties kept the opposition silent, at least in public.

The added fields of study and the new athletic programs required investment in new facilities, an enlarged and updated science center, an indoor track and tennis building, and Olympic-size outdoor track and field facilities. The buildup to a major fundraising campaign converts even the most peaceable campus into a hotbed of seething political rivalries, as disciplines and programs compete for resources, usually in a long-drawn-out and often inconclusive process. I knew there wasn't time for that. And I wasn't sure the usual process would produce the right decisions.

We needed quick action to position us well for the lean years. The trouble was that although faculty and trustees want to establish planning priorities for their institution, the only person who really holds all the necessary information about both internal and external environments in her or his head is the president. Yet, for political reasons, neither group can permit itself to be seen as abdicating judgment to the president.

After an all-day trustee retreat devoted to planning issues, the Board encouraged me to develop my own strategic plan and worry about how to get it accepted later. Coincidentally, I was to take sabbatical leave that summer and fall, so I developed the ten-year plan for Smith covering every function and discipline, indicating the funding necessary year by year to implement it, and the necessary steps to raise it. Then I departed for five months, leaving the Board and the College Planning and Resources Committee to review and amend it. While I was luxuriating in working on writing again, free to play with my own ideas rather than define academic policy, the campus was deprived of the executive leader as a target for criticism or challenge. Both groups faced up to the issues, bought the plan concepts and goals, and accepted them, changing the language but not the component parts.

Once I returned, the formal approvals came speedily. I had billed what was a major shift in capital allocation, and the largest single investment in facilities in the college's history, as positioning for the enrollment downturn, so the scope of the changes wasn't apparent to many, and the focus on competing as an avowedly modern feminist institution was launched without major controversy.

It was possible to make such ambitious plans because the Board and the Alumnae Association had strong leaders in the 1980s who understood that Smith's operations were running smoothly and that my focus was shifting toward the strategic questions for the future. Kathleen Bell, a career diplomat who'd reached ambassadorial rank representing the United States at Unesco, wasn't fazed by managing many different competing interests. "Jill," she said briskly, "you get on with carrying out your program and leave me to manage the relationship with the Board and build bridges to the faculty." She did so with such charming and effortless efficiency that I hardly noticed the way governance flowed so serenely until her retirement. Nancy Lange, who led the Alumnae Association, was another professional volunteer with a talent for strategic thinking. She excelled at planning the way each segment of her constituency should be educated about the steps necessary to keep Smith highly competitive in the nineties. And Joan Lane, who chaired the Board in my last three years, brought the perspective of a larger university to Smith's affairs. She and her husband were deeply involved in the affairs of Stanford, and she worked on development in Stanford's Faculty of Arts and Sciences. We'd become longtime partners in Smith fundraising when she shepherded me up and down the California coast during Smith's fund drive, always managing to deliver me to call on a key donor at exactly the appointed time. Because of her skill and experience as a fundraiser, she helped me educate the Board on the scale and professional talent needed to increase Smith's fundraising capability. It was easy to get people to think big with a trustee leader who wasn't afraid to set large fundraising goals, and who communicated her assurance to colleagues.

This happy outcome gave me the chance to act decisively in what I'd already determined should be my last three years in the job. I needed to figure out the size of the bond issue necessary to get the facilities plan started, set the necessary college groups to work on building plans, work out the schedule of the cash flow, and estimate what capital could be raised to seed all the projects in advance of the major campaign that should follow the appointment of my successor.

Once my private date for stepping down was announced, I would have a great fundraising platform: asking donors to help me leave a hefty part of the funding raised for my successor.

It intensified the pleasure of my working days to see the lineaments of a first-rate athletic facility emerging, and to watch the drainage project that prepared for the installation of an Olympic-size outdoor track on what had been a soggy and little-used series of hockey and lacrosse fields.

There were other competitive positioning tasks that were less well received and less painlessly implemented. I needed to force recognition of the changing higher-educational environment on a faculty still complacent in the belief that students were lucky to be accepted at Smith and ought to know as high school applicants its history, high academic standards, and distinguished faculty. Beneath this complacency was a taboo on marketing Smith. To admit that there could be successful competitors required admitting that one's own academic offerings might not be the most dazzling available. And once the idea that one's courses and curriculum had to appeal to students was entertained, the lordly notion of the scholar was undermined and the service aspects of education were emphasized. Marketing was seen as a commercial activity, which polluted the purity of the academic's role, and anyone who advocated it was dismissed as a crass proponent of the corporate mentality ready to reduce education to a commodity.

That was why more good administrative careers had been ruined by college-image studies than by failing football teams. But we had to undertake one and learn more about our market perception. My task was ensured success when we found an alumna graduate of the sixties who was the head of marketing at a major consumer products company and was happy to volunteer her time to oversee the image study and help us come up with a marketing plan that was appropriate for Smith.

We began to make some headway when we showed faculty films of focus groups with seventeen-year-olds and their parents from different regions of the country discussing college selection. In Texas or California, outside major urban centers few had ever heard of Smith, and when shown its logo thought the image of Sophia, the goddess of knowledge, indicated a Catholic women's college. Parents who had heard of Smith didn't want their daughters to attend, because they thought they would turn instantly into Betty Friedan or Gloria Steinem. The fact that Nancy Reagan and Barbara Bush were also alumnae had never registered. Every way the future college student encountered Smith—Viewbook, Course Catalogue, admissions applications—shouted "OLD-FASHIONED AND STUFFY."

The course descriptions in the catalogue produced yawns among young people raised on MTV, and our cherished photographs of ivy-covered buildings said "traditional, upper-class, not for me." We changed the logo, filled the promotional materials with images of fall and spring, rewrote the course descriptions, and introduced color into the print materials. This made sense to a Board of Trustees well aware of the cultural bridges that had to be built between Smith and potential applicants, but it enraged faculty conservatives, many of whom secreted caches of the old letterhead and stubbornly refused to use the new designs. The changes were all attributed to Jill's "commercialism," which was undermining everything of value in Smith's history. But they worked.

An even tougher taboo to break was the value system enshrined in the financial aid office. People who give away money to those in need become arrogant, just by the nature of the task and the power they hold. And the arrogance was reinforced by the close-knit nature of the financial aid fraternity in highly selective colleges. The values built into the federal system, and into the allocation of the college or university's aid and loan grants, were set by administrators whose lives had been shaped by the Great Depression. Families who carried significant levels of debt were classified as thriftless and were refused aid, regardless of whether it made financial sense to finance many family expenditures through debt, as it did in periods of very high inflation in the late seventies and early eighties. Judgments about families and their capacity to repay loans governed, though we all knew that in most instances parents passed on the debt to students and expected them to earn the loan installments both during and after college. Everyone had to be treated with cookie-cutter uniformity, even when it disadvantaged the institution, because to deviate from the common practice was to lose face among financial aid confreres. Yet granting the same level of aid to students regardless of academic ability guaranteed that one would inflate one's applicant pool with less-qualified people, because the odds of getting in and receiving substantial aid were higher there than in schools that gave more aid to better-qualified students. I won the battle to change, but with considerable acrimony.

I had many cross conversations with the Director of Financial Aid. We were a service organization. Why did it take so long to process aid applications? It riled people we wanted to think well of Smith. Eventually, a simple loan-calculation package was installed on the Financial Aid Office's computer system, and we could tell people what to expect when they made their first telephone inquiry.

Our worst disagreements were over value judgments about families and their financial arrangements. I wanted to know why a bright African-American student hadn't been offered aid. "Look at the family's debt" was the response. "Even their furniture is rented. They're aspiring to a lifestyle they can't afford." I said it probably made sense to rent furniture in this family's circumstances, and anyway it was none of our business. We wanted to find reasons to admit students, not to turn them down.

I also got into trouble from time to time by sending the family of a bright African-American or Hispanic applicant from a rural setting or an urban ghetto the money to come to visit the college, so they could see the place their daughter would be living. "You're treating people differently" was the refrain. But I knew those families faced a different set of challenges in deciding about a college for their daughter. Smith was an unknown WASP world, and we needed to let the family see it before they made their choice.

Then there was the increasing problem of the child of divorced parents, one of whom refused to submit family financial information for the daughter's loan application. I thought we had to recognize the fact of single-parent families and not disadvantage the child because one parent was irresponsible. That was a battle I didn't win, though we did become more flexible about recognizing that some families didn't even know where the supposedly responsible parent was.

One of the sources of my confidence about recognizing the service nature of our mission and using the discipline of marketing was that I'd gained a window on other kinds of organizations through service on a variety of boards. I chose them to teach me something I needed to know. The IBM World Trade Corporation because it kept me in touch with Canada and Australian higher education through IBM's university relationships, and because I learned at the source about the ways information technology was transforming the world and could have profound impact on the transfer of knowledge in the classroom. That understanding made me raise the money to pay the entire faculty to spend time in workshops on computing and pedagogy. Merrill Lynch helped me gain perspective on the management of our endowment and the economic environment in which we operated. The College Retirement Equities Fund—part of the institution that managed pension assets for America's private schools and higher educational institutions—gave me insight into the demography of the academic profession, the factors that influence retirement choices, and the changing nature of retirement lifestyles. That was critical knowledge for me at Smith, because we had a very large cohort of faculty in their late fifties and early sixties whose presence limited our ability to hire young, recently trained faculty in new disciplines or new fields within established disciplines. The TIAA-CREF staff, a faculty committee, and some knowledgeable trustees helped us invent a phased retirement plan that enabled us to move some of the aging cohort into early retirement without significant reduction of benefits. Smith was then free to reorient its curriculum to the needs of the 1980s.

All three—IBM, Merrill Lynch, and CREF—gave me another perspective on the way different organizations dealt with their human capital and interacted with their clientele. Each one was an education in management, a continuing seminar in economics. The fresh perspectives they provided enabled me to look at Smith's management issues from many different angles, instead of accepting the ways of the academy as received wisdom. The broader perspectives didn't make me popular with faculty or administrative staff, but they helped me get things done.

I found that even the higher-education associations, where board service was a duty, gave me enlarged perspectives on the job. It was an education for someone not native to the United States to be coached on the intricacies of higher-education loan legislation by a superprofessional staff at the Consortium on Financing Higher Education, and then be piloted through the rituals of testimony to House and Senate Committees. It boggled my mind to see how the national government really worked, with House, Senate, and executive branch each pushing its own scheme on higher-education financing, until the last moment when suddenly the compromise was put together.

State educational politics were a puzzle of another sort. In Massachusetts, public and private systems were approximately equal in size, and the task of lobbying to secure improved state financial aid required a delicate minuet, carefully choreographed in private so the heads of public and private institutions didn't trip over one another. I loved the juicy ethnic mix of Massachusetts politics. Boston's Irish Mafia constantly reminded me of the Irish in Australian political life—the rhetoric and invective flowed in a different accent but the passion and the genius for political maneuvering were the same. I believed public and private systems had complementary goals, and enjoyed seeing how well we could jointly manage the state financial aid commitments. The biggest win for me came when we persuaded the Commonwealth to continue welfare support for able women who won financial aid grants from private colleges. The victory was brief, a victim of the mean-spirited attacks on the welfare system of the nineties, but while it lasted the results gave us welfare mothers who became lawyers, clergywomen, management experts, painters, poets, and passionately committed schoolteachers. Those concerned about the cost to the state government could take comfort in the fact that a few years' investment in their minds was quickly repaid by the taxes they paid in their subsequent careers.

Another joy in life was the chance to take on more teaching. My schedule had become too erratic to manage regular classroom appearances. But I found the perfect partner to teach with in Susan Bourque of the Government Department. We taught a series of courses on women and politics, which, added to the occasional honors seminar in history for the History Department, meant that I saw a much wider group of students in the classroom. I'd always enjoyed lecturing, and I graded my lectures by how far I could get in any lecture hour before students began asking questions and the class turned into a conversation. The Women and Politics course attracted a strong contingent of athletes, so I'd see the crew and the swim team hard at their training when I went to the gym at six-thirty for my morning swim, and then encounter them again in class at eleven. Nothing clarifies the mind like the pleasure of brainstorming with colleagues about how to get complex ideas across to students, so the planning and preparation of a jointly taught course is half the pleasure. Susie's background was in politics and anthropology and specifically the study of indigenous rural people in Peru. Mine was in nineteenth- and twentieth-century American social history, so each issue discussed on women's notions of citizenship and political participation could be treated in comparative perspective. Those hours in the classroom were like lustral waters to an academic turned administrator. They washed away all the clutter of managing a complex institution, and they put students and their learning back at the center of things.

And I enjoyed Smith students intensely. With a lifetime of teaching behind me, I knew each generation of students presents different challenges. Students of the sixties and seventies were intensely political, and near oblivious to humanistic universals. Students of the eighties were focused on careers and professions but were also able to approach universal humanistic questions via non-Western cultures. I was lucky to be teaching very bright students just before the burgeoning of postmodern cultural criticism required reconsidering history and narrative and ignited the culture wars that raged in the nineties about the abandonment of the Western worldview.

Smith's faculty conservatives bewailed the changes in intellectual fashion and recalled what they remembered as a brighter student generation in a mythical golden past. I never agreed with them. We go through periods when educational institutions are in synchrony with the questions that matter to the young, and periods where there is a real mismatch between institution and generational issues. I thought faculty demography accounted for a lot of the carping about student interests and achievement. Smith, like all its peer institutions, had an aging faculty, recruited in the late fifties and early sixties, somewhat out of touch with students often younger than the complaining faculty members' children. For me, no matter what the harmony or disharmony of institution and students, the curiosity of the intelligent young about the world they seek to understand is invariably stimulating, funny, irreverent, and not infrequently very beautiful. I never accepted the American obsession with SATs and standardized testing and found the range of talents in my Smith classroom just about the same as the ones I'd encountered twenty or thirty years earlier.

A particularly treasured spot was the research center on women established in 1978, and by the mid-eighties beginning to build up an endowment to ensure its continuation. It was the brainchild of my happiest set of intellectual friendships at Smith. I remembered beginning to ask questions about governing theories of the female psyche and social role while an undergraduate in the 1950s. And I recalled the dismissive way my own graduate research had been treated by colleagues in the early sixties. I'd then thought I was a pioneer in research on women's history, only to discover that there had been an entire generation of women scholars working on the sociology, history, and psychology of sex roles in the 1920s and '30s. Their work was out of print and had been virtually unknown to me a mere thirty years later. So my dream was to found at Smith a center for research on women's experience, which would be endowed, would ensure a collective memory, and could go on generating knowledge no matter what the intellectual fashions of the moment and the objectives of the agencies that funded scholarship.

My dream was a nightmare for many faculty and some trustees. Most faculty had chosen college teaching to escape the research imperatives of major universities. Trustees feared the cost of endowing an activity not directly related to undergraduate teaching, and many were worried about seeming to mingle Smith's identity with the feminist scholarship of a particular generation. A gifted group of faculty from Government, Economics, Psychology, and Education came up with the design and governance of a research center so open to the interests of all liberal arts faculty that it became merely one more resource for supporting faculty scholarship. Once established, they set quietly about building its donor base, aided by the leadership of a group of feminist alumnae. I'd missed the intense pleasure of graduate teaching, the mentoring of professional scholars in the making. Smith's Project on Women and Social Change, through its conferences reporting research and identifying the most productive areas for future work, gave me back the sense of building a field of study and helping to foster a new scholarly generation.

But it was not all clear sailing. I had some sharp disagreements with trustees as the political environment shifted to the right, over invitations to speakers, the granting of honors, lesbian rights—all subjects on which I felt it impossible to yield to new-right attitudes and values. These were minor in the context of a decade of tireless support, but they made me ponder the future and the question of what was the right platform from which to serve the causes I believed in, given the sharp shift in the political climate.

These were minor eddies in a strong current of success toward the goals I'd set on arriving at Smith. But beneath the surface, there was a strong undertow pulling me toward more profound existential issues. My mother's death had been unbearably sad. An undetected brain tumor caused her behavior to become more and more erratic and paranoid. Wrongly diagnosed as a case of early dementia accentuated by overmedication, she died of the stroke brought on by the brain tumor, lonely and at odds with both her surviving children. I found the experience of closing up her house and beginning the settlement of her estate a sorrow I knew I'd live with permanently. She had been so brave and beautiful when young, and she died raging at a fate she'd done much to bring on herself, through refusal of medical care. My relationship with her, no matter how attenuated at the end, had been the shaping force of my early life. I walked like her, smiled like her, drew my passion for knowledge from her. My hands had the same bony joints and freckles in exactly the same places. And we'd not made peace.

John's peripheral neuropathy, from which he inched painfully slowly toward recovery, and the regular, dreadfully predictable anniversary bouts of mania, followed by depression, emphasized the fragility of life and the fleeting nature of happiness. My admiration for the way he handled illness and the unremitting courage with which he fought for life and health made worldly success seem useful but not emotionally of great resonance. I knew there were things, never to be recorded on any curriculum vitae, that undergirded a whole life.

And then as I came to my fiftieth year, I realized that I was approaching the age at which my father died. He'd been dead for forty years, but my memory of him and of his loss grew clearer with age, and kept me alert to last things. Each year as the anniversary of his death approached, I'd wake one morning stomach gripped with anxiety, waves of despair washing over me, sliding inexorably into bleak depression. What's the matter with me? I'd wonder. And then I'd realize that the calendar was moving toward December 9. The blackness made me hate the mindless merriment of Christmas. I was lucky John agreed with me that the current commercial form of Christmas was a dubious gift from Britain's Hanoverian sovereigns. In the brief spells of our private life when we weren't responsible for institutional celebrations, we'd have a shrimp salad and a glass of champagne for our Christmas feast and spend the day taking long walks in the country or reading the season's new books. December was a bad month in general, because John's mania frequently hit the week before Christmas, often in a form that required a week or so in psychiatric care. At those times, I'd wait eagerly for the campus to empty, and the last Christmas crowd to disperse, to be alone by the fire with my companionable cat and the quiet I needed for reflection on the paradox of public success and private sadness.

Moving toward my tenth year at Smith, I felt an intense longing to live in another self. My drive had switched suddenly toward the creative, while my current life was managerial. I was writing measured memoranda to the Board of Trustees when what wanted to come out was words, poetry, imagery, intimations of the numinous rather than budget projections. I seemed suddenly to have arrived at a point in life where the role of universal caregiver was no longer tolerable. I was impatient with endless meetings, less amused by student and faculty foibles, and sure someone new could do a better job. I was restless because the words I wanted to write came pushing insistently—on long drives, while jogging around the campus, just before sleep. In the past, I'd been able to put them off—wait till I'd climbed this hill, achieved that goal. Now it was as if some friendly guardian angel had come by College Hall and told me to get going.

7

THE POLITICS OF
WOMEN'S EDUCATION

✹ ABOUT EIGHTEEN MONTHS BEFORE the end of my second term, I'd confirmed for the Chairman of Smith's Board my decision that I wouldn't be seeking to extend it beyond June 1985. Once that was settled, I began to think about what I'd learned from the experience of running a women's educational institution and what I wanted to think about in a future uncluttered by administrative detail.

Most feminist analysis came from the point of view of women working within male-led organizations. They were looking out at a male-controlled world from the often shaky platform of seeking to change it by persuasion, or by confrontation unsupported by a strong, unified constituency. Smith had a predominantly female Board of Trustees, its living alumnae were 40,000 enthusiastic women, and its undergraduate student body was another three thousand exuberant young adult women. That meant that I'd been seeing the world from the unique perspective of social territory I thought I'd brought to be controlled by and for women. Of course it still had to operate in the context of a male-controlled society, but its mission was now keyed to contemporary women and their needs, not to what others, usually male, thought would be good for them. The process of getting to that point was a continuing seminar on the politics of women's education.

I learned most from the face we presented to the world and the way the institution was perceived. Spending the better part of a decade as a spokeswoman on women questions—women and work, women and religion, women in academe, women in the third world, women in the arts, women and voluntarism—I had found all the usual reductive tags journalists and politicians used very instructive. The "women and" questions came because the questioners couldn't be bothered to think at a more precise level about what they wanted to know. Answering all those questions forced me to articulate positions on many issues that had never come up in my academic life. At Smith they came up almost daily, and I soon learned that my answer was delivered into a highly charged political environment. They might sound like questions in the abstract, but they were asked to advance a point of view in the tiresome and seemingly never-ending, repetitive discussion of women's place—what the French, since early modern times, had been calling the *querelle des femmes*. It was repetitive because women lacked a power base from which to drive change, and because of the cultural insistence on defining women only in terms of their sexual and reproductive functions.

Answering questions from politicians or corporate leaders on standard feminist goals—equal pay, for instance—taught me that most people thought about women's advancement as a zero-sum game. If women gained equal pay, there would be less for men. No one considered the fact that better use of women's talents would be a source of productivity. To most people, changing the segregated workforce and giving women opportunities to learn and advance over a lifetime career wasn't a productivity issue, it was just a transaction in a zero-sum game. I'd try to get people to see how the abolition of slavery and a free market for labor had enhanced productivity in earlier stages of capitalism, and what would be lost in the emerging knowledge-based society if women's intellectual abilities were underutilized. But it was a hard point to get across to people who saw women as unskilled labor or helpful middle-class wives. I realized that feminists hadn't painted a very good picture of the kind of world we'd live in if women succeeded in winning every plank of the Western feminist platform. Science fiction by women was the closest we had to utopian thinking, but it wasn't much help on the zero-sum issue. We didn't even have many Bildungsromans by women that weren't just about sexual adventures. I decided that when my time was free, I'd write one.

Never a doctrinaire liberal, I realized the shallowness of much liberal rhetoric on the subject of women and equality. It never puzzled me for a moment that African-Americans and other minorities rejected assimilation as a goal, because it was an invitation to believe oneself equal in a world where white males controlled all the gateways to opportunity and were blissfully unconscious of the bias built into their assessments of talent and potential. It didn't help that women, in particular, waited to be recognized instead of insisting on recognition. I was astonished that they did that even in a women's institution. But simple assimilation was hard to manage anywhere in society, because women who modeled male conduct were seen as aggressive, and those who were quietly efficient were seen as not forceful enough. My conversation often stumbled over the puzzled question about why women would want to be educated separately, and why I, who my questioner clearly thought competent, would want to run a women's "school."

The subtext of the question was that women could not possibly have any intellectual reason for being together. The life of the mind was a male activity to which women were lucky to be admitted. They were great research assistants, but the conversation about knowledge was in a male voice. So if women chose to be educated separately from men, their reasons couldn't be intellectual—they must be sexual and involve sexual rejection of males. Invariably, the discussion then got around to homophobic subjects on which all vestiges of liberal tolerance for difference vanished. I had a hard time explaining the concept of parallel institutions for men and women at different life stages, and never managed to convey the possibility that liberty might be greater in a society of greater complexity than in one of uniformity. So far as women's life of the mind went, I could see that there weren't any female counterparts to the classic male stories of an education. There was nothing I could refer people to. No female Franklins. No sister for Henry Adams. I decided that that was another blank page to fill. Just as soon as I had time, I'd try to write a lively picture of the way a woman's mind developed and how her intellectual vocation was formed.

What was startling was how worried people got over any grouping of women without men. It troubled people to think of women owning and running their own turf. It troubled men faced with critical wives, mothers, or daughters. It also troubled insecure women uncertain of what life would be like if they had to earn their own way in the world. It couldn't be normal. Ergo it was deviant, and since women were defined by their bodies and not their minds and talents, it had to be sexually deviant, and the course of study had to be intellectually weak.

One of the greatest gifts I received from Smith was that many of my own assumptions had to be questioned and revised through the experience of a female-controlled organization. Like all women making their way into a professional world, I'd grown up thinking of women's voluntarism as a compensation for living outside the public sphere. But meeting and working with Smith's managerial volunteers, some of whom headed large organizations, taught me that given the difficulties of moving beyond helping roles in male-led organizations, smart women just founded their own organizations to do what they wanted in urban politics, or environmental reform, or education. It was a quicker route to power and influence, and it made pragmatic sense. It was a tactical rather than a strategic approach, but a very effective one. Later, I'd see businesswomen, tired of being overlooked in large corporations, settle for running their own small business.

These were both sound tactics at the individual level, but I was more interested in the strategic question of changing core institutions. I felt that by the end of my decade at Smith, I'd have done my time in the academy. Now that the political climate was shifting to the right, it seemed that the most receptive environment for change was the business world, where government-mandated affirmative action programs had required the employment of qualified women. I decided that I'd give more time to corporate governance, and that I'd use what I'd learned about managing nonprofits to work on broader educational issues involving people much less privileged than the Smith student body.

I'd grown up thinking homophobia a redneck reaction of the undereducated, but I met it daily from highly educated professionals, male and female, and from all places in the political spectrum. People who worried about all-female groups had a lively fantasy life about homosexuality, made more active by the political turmoil within the feminist movement in the seventies and eighties, during which one segment of the movement rejected heterosexuality on political grounds. I didn't see all forms of oppression in the world caused by the gender system, but defending the right of lesbian women to exist, and to be teachers and students, was a tough political task that showed me an ugly face of bias I simply hadn't seen before. I could tell exactly when the subject was about to come up in just about any conversation. The questioner would hunch his or her shoulders, lean forward confidentially, and in a lowered voice ask, "What are you going to do about all those lesbians at Smith?" The questioner always seemed to believe I could wave a wand and purge this beleaguered minority from the campus.

I had three answers, none of which ever satisfied the questioners. I'd say that homosexuality was a universal present in all societies we knew and was no more or less present at Smith than in any similar institution. It was a fact of life that the questioner should accept. What Smith educated was people's minds, and their sexuality was no business of our administration, which should be evaluating people in terms of their intellectual achievement. That answer didn't satisfy. Then I'd ask if the questioner thought there were any gay male faculty and students at Harvard, Yale, or Dartmouth (the most common affiliations of my questioners). "Of course," they would respond. Did they think the presidents of Harvard, Yale, or Dartmouth should be spending their time policing the sex life of their students and faculty? The questioner would have to admit that she or he thought about male sexuality differently. What young men did was their own business, but society still had ownership in women's sexuality and should control it. It was always an illuminating conversation, and it converted my standard liberal commitment to tolerance to a passionate defense of gay rights, because I came to see those rights as fundamental feminist issues. They were part of the fight for women to own every aspect of themselves and not to be a form of property.

Most overworked and harried college and university presidents don't see their position as powerful, but I soon learned that to most people it was. I never gave an interview to a journalist or talked to an alumnae group without being asked, "What's it like to be a woman in power?" Moreover, the contemporary feminist movement had defined the quest for power as a "male hangup," a psychological obsession caused by Western definitions of machismo. In that school of feminist thought, only women were believed to be sane about power.

They didn't seek to rule and took action exclusively based on consensus. To do anything else was to have sold out to male values and embarked on an "ego trip."

It was a point of view I'd never agreed with. The Greek political ideas that undergirded democratic institutions might have come from a society that excluded women from the polis, but the fact of their exclusion or inclusion didn't make the central political issue of power and its just limits any different. To me, the argument for including women was one of equity and utility, not some biologically based transformative capacity. I thought the executive role very little modified by the sex of the person who played it. There could be lots of challenge and contention about lower-level management positions, but institutions stand or fall by the quality of their executive leadership, and all but the deeply disaffected are ready to concede that. Did I enjoy it? Was my ego enlarged by it? The answer to both was: of course. We are all transformed by the institutions we lead and by the experience of final decision making, however large or small the span of authority. That role and the tasks that go with it require a degree of self-scrutiny that most of us, female or male, rarely undertake. The person who sits at the point where many contending interests clash, and has to decide how to manage the conflict in a way that serves the greater public interest, is educated and changed by the experience.

Institutions exist in and are legitimated by the larger society, so communication about Smith to its external publics—government, funders of higher education, learned societies, women's organizations—gave me a sense of speaking to a larger audience than I'd had as an academic historian, and in the process I was given a practical education on public policy issues I'd known only theoretically before. That larger audience eventually gave me a different voice and an entitlement to speak on many more subjects than just historical ones, and that changed what I wanted to write and think about. So I learned firsthand that the supposed problem of women's public voice is a function of whom they speak to and not of their biology.

When I wrote about nineteenth-century Western women, I was always careful to point out that they participated in technological innovation until the development of formal engineering training. The Frenchwomen who wanted to join the army of the Republic to help defend the French Revolution didn't need technical training to understand the use of pikes and swords. On the domestic front, women designed many improvements in household technology. The Shakers designed elegant solutions to cleaning and to managing household space. Under the pressure of the disappearance of a servant class in nineteenth-century America, Catherine Beecher had come up with an early design for a washing machine. But as engineering became a formal male profession, women fell silent on the subject of technology, except to bewail the lost craft tradition of female health care, or to dream about technology in utopian terms.

It was hard work trying to get trustees and faculty at Smith to see the importance of technological education for women. The whole question of women's control of and ability to shape the material context of life didn't seem real to them, though to me it was a crucial political issue. There were one or two women faculty allies— physicists and mathematicians whose hard work made possible the development of a dual-degree program in engineering at Smith in partnership with the University of Massachusetts—but the time demands of meeting two sets of requirements meant that only the most dedicated undergraduates took up the opportunity. We produced field geologists and architects, but Smith wasn't an environment to stimulate the technological imagination. It was a problem I didn't solve, except to insist on computer science as an important field of study. I needed a better education on technology myself, and made it a goal for the next decade. John had already decided that Boston was where he wanted to live, so I began some quiet conversations about how I could be affiliated with MIT. Time to read and think would be like water after a desert trek, and I knew I was getting close to the oasis.

I wasn't interested in debunking technology and the engineering mentality. A childhood without electricity or gas, daily struggles with quirky wood stoves and outdoor privies, taught me to value the machine. I'd also watched daily the force and manipulation associated with the domestication of animals. And I'd had my own vivid demonstration of how any form of farming or domestication of animals disrupts nature. So I was impatient with the feminist vogue for worship of the mother goddess and the accompanying idealization of early agricultural societies. My feminist friends who thought such societies nonintrusive on nature had never seen a horse broken or a stallion gelded or looked at an overgrazed pasture.

But nonetheless, I learned a lot from the Smith alumnae involved in environmental organizations, the students who studied genetically engineered crops, and even the sentimental feminist faculty who bought the idea that women were the defenders of the planet against marauding male exploiters of natural resources. They made me think about who was responsible for desertification in Africa and the destruction of equatorial forests. I knew my own family had played its part in the environmental decline of our Australian grasslands, so I had firsthand experience to bring to environmental issues. I didn't see the global phenomenon of migration as the result of gender politics. It was a demographic event to be sure, and it was producing a heavier and heavier draw on the world's natural resources. But I thought that women like me who drove cars and lived in air-conditioned buildings were as much a part of the problem as men. To me, the sentimental view of women as protectors of nature ignored larger questions of demography and ecological balance, and overlooked the fact that the idea of nature itself was a cultural variable. My humanistic education had left the human/nonhuman boundary and relationship unexamined. I decided one of my midlife tasks would be to educate myself about ecofeminism and its critics.

One thing I was sure I wouldn't do was spend more time on the study of feminist theory. I was happy to read the occasional analysis of semiotics, linguistics, and gender. I was instructed by feminist literary criticism, and enlightened by feminist analysis of the treatment of the nude in Western art, but I wasn't attracted to endless semitheological discussions conducted in abstruse language by a small, self-involved scholarly community of feminist theorists. Theory was, of course, the ultimate key to understanding, but it was only valuable to me when expressed with elegant clarity in a way that could be understood by the noninitiate. It seemed to me that some current feminist theoretical battles came very close to arguing about how many angels could dance on the head of a pin. I was an activist at heart. It mattered more to me to get better education and broader awareness and concern about the desperate material problems of women in non-Western countries than to understand the last nuance about the female and alterity in Western culture.

Internally, the politics of knowledge at Smith had revolved around the study of women and the study of non-Western fields. Conservatives claimed that the Western humanistic tradition should not be eroded by "relativistic" studies of other cultures. Why build language programs in Chinese and Japanese when students needed first to know Greek and Latin? Why spend so much effort on Buddhist studies when no one read the King James Bible anymore? Every cultural conservative could understand teaching Hebrew to understand Biblical texts, but Arabic? Why that, when there were no longer many students who could write a sentence in English that parsed? At issue was the question of whether or not the world should be seen, both in time and in cultural expression, from a Western European point of view, or even whether it was possible to construe reality from a central point. Hence the bitter battles about the abandonment of Western civilization courses, and the skirmishes about whether the voyages of European exploration should be seen from the point of view of the European adventurers or from that of the indigenous peoples of the various continents on which they settled.

This was the political battle of ideas that inspired the new right and gave birth to the leftish postmodern view of cultural politics. Its resonance at Smith was complicated by the gender composition of the faculty, because deconstructing the narrative of European superiority also undermined the concept of the Western male hero. So a curriculum committee could become heated over a simple question such as to whether a course treating women's contribution to the French Resistance in the Second World War was biased or not. Proponents of the course would argue that it was odd that the widespread and well-documented participation of women in the Resistance should somehow not have made its way into histories of the period, and opponents would see the proposal as a feminist effort to devalue the Jean Moulins of the maquis.

Possibly even more inflammatory were the efforts to insert works by women into the canon of Western art and literature. These battles were standoffs during the 1980s, dealt with by academic eclecticism and the approval of courses representative of both contending points of view. So a Smith student arriving in 1975 might have found herself reading only works by great male writers in 1975, whereas by 1985 she could choose either works by those cheerfully referred to as "dead white males" or she could settle for women writers from George Eliot to Toni Morrison, or both. The solution was a costly addition to the mounting of the curriculum, and troublesome or not depending on whether one thought the young should create their own synthetic view of culture or have one offered to them. The eclecticism didn't bother me. It was symptomatic of a major paradigm shift in the idea of high culture, and in geopolitics. I didn't expect it to be worked out in my lifetime. I remembered how long it took Oxford and Cambridge to accept the idea of teaching modern history, an intellectual shift that took more than a quarter century. And I was confident students were bright enough to figure out the politics once they were alerted to the male bias in the canon.

The battles were different in the social sciences, because the mode of participant observation built into sociology and anthropology had created a disciplinary oeuvre that rested upon total failure to observe the roles of women in non-Western cultures, or if they were observed, to interpret them correctly. So the early anthropologists who were the giants in the field, like Malinowski, had simply concluded, for example, that Australian Aboriginal women had no role in religion, because their rituals were secret and not revealed to men. Correcting this sort of misconception was not just a matter of inserting existing materials into the curriculum but required remaking the discipline. And sociologists like the eminent Talcott Parsons, who had structured gender concepts on the divide between instrumental and expressive behavior, could not be dealt with by just adding in supplementary texts. The remedy was rethinking how bias shapes participant observation, and why such dualistic concepts once seemed to have such explanatory power. Because their disciplines were based on comparative studies, which require some relativistic assessment, it was easier for the social scientists to adapt. A Smith student who arrived in 1975 would have been given the entire orthodoxy on women's closeness to nature and subordinate role in religious ritual in the introductory courses to social science disciplines, but by 1985 she'd find both points of view and their historical origins explained in her introductory course, and a set of upper-level courses drawing on trailblazing feminist research.

The change wasn't so easy in economics and political science.

Since economics is based on measuring what can be counted in human productivity, and all the elegant mathematical theorems of neoclassical economics rest on monetary measures, it's more difficult to adjust for the fact that women's unpaid work is in fact part of a society's productivity. And the founding documents of political theory are, of course, based on the great texts drawn from Greek political culture, which didn't see women as part of the polis. Here, as in the humanities, various forms of parallel curriculum evolved, leaving the student to reach her own conclusions. But the going was harder for young feminist scholars in these fields. Their research had to be better, their conclusions more rigorous, and their professional standing more broadly recognized in order for them to earn a permanent place on the Smith faculty. So students in the 1980s might find all counter views of political theory or economics taught, but more often than not by a rotating crop of younger, untenured scholars.

And if they went on to elite graduate schools, they would be caught in the crossfire of these disciplinary battles, which were totally unresolved. Certainly if they attended the major scholarly conventions of the learned societies in the social sciences, they would find research that dealt with women ghettoized in separate segments of the program, whereas in the context of a women's liberal arts college they'd have seen efforts to integrate feminist scholarship within disciplinary boundaries, albeit by relatively junior faculty.

In the natural sciences, the political issues hinged on the philosophy and sociology of Western science. The philosophical question hinged on the methods of science, the effort to break down living organisms into ever smaller units for the purpose of control and manipulation. Or in one manifestation of physics, to develop ever more destructive weapons for military purposes. And both, of course, offered unlimited potential for unintended consequences damaging to ecological balance.

These critiques, by no means exclusively feminist, had special resonance in a women's college because of the sociology of Western science, based on a culture organized since the seventeenth century to exclude women participants. Since Smith women wanted to be prepared for advanced study in all fields, the curricular response was to build an ever more preprofessional science curriculum while addressing the philosophical and sociological issues through courses on the history and philosophy of science. It was a pragmatic fix that worked, since the reorientation of science as an enterprise required resources and facilities well beyond the range of an undergraduate science program. It also worked because it was on the applications of science that feminist perspectives could most easily be brought to bear. What was glaringly missing in the curriculum was a multidisciplinary environmental studies program, where feminist perspectives were clearly relevant. But this was a project left for my successor.

Of course there was a vigorous right-wing backlash within the general academic culture of the 1990s to all these critiques of established disciplines, as there was to the effort to create undergraduate communities where different ethnic, gender, and sexual-preference groups were not demeaned by hostile or prejudiced majorities. I thought the rancor and emotional excess of the backlash a sign of the power of the efforts to redefine "official" knowledge. And since I believed with Hegel that the advancement of knowledge was a dialectical process, I thought the political passions were at least a sign of engagement rather than neglect.

The new-right backlash seemed to me prompted by the extraordinary degree to which feminist criticism of patriarchal values had succeeded. The Vietnam War had certainly helped to undermine within American culture military values already called into question in Europe by the experience of two world wars—and as always with extremes of cultural rebellion, much of value inherited from the classical tradition of courage, valor, and honor had also been discredited.

Feminist critiques of male values had thus occurred in a very receptive environment, to which the right-wing backlash was a predictable response.

The spirited criticism of the excesses of feminist scholarship, therefore, seemed to me entirely to be expected, especially as a new generation of women benefitted from the successes of the sixties and seventies, which had opened many opportunities and removed many economic, political, and educational barriers for women. But I thought the sentimental view of the female—which emphasized maternal bonding, blurred or permeable boundaries to the female personality, and intuitive versus rational knowledge—was proving attractive to the rising generation of young women eager to mute or call a truce in the gender wars as they tried to make their way in professional life and business. The problem was that such a definition left out the rationale and institutional framework for women's intellectual life, something still quite problematic in many areas of scholarly inquiry, and something of critical importance for the future.

But I knew I wasn't going to be fighting those battles on university campuses in the years ahead. I wanted to move on to create texts rather than study them. The new knowledge I was looking for was about environmental change, and the question of gendered perceptions of nature, something not yet roiling the debates of Smith's curriculum committees, or figuring prominently in Western feminist discourse.

Smith had definitely made my theoretical historical understanding of gender politics three-dimensional. But there was no question that I needed time to move on, to think more about the pluses and minuses of where we'd arrived in the gender politics of my day. I needed time out for more training, a better coach on vital issues like technology and environmental hazards, and a new arena for the fight.

I hadn't expected the next round for me to be literary, but that was where all my inner voices were leading me. And watching generations of young women grow intellectually, discover intellectual vocations, and begin to take charge of their lives had been a powerful experience. I couldn't find that women's story written about much except in pop culture terms by movie stars and rock singers. We clearly needed more writers who could make the serious woman intellectual's life experience come alive for both women and men. So that would be an early assignment for my new life.

It would be very different operating again without the base of a strong feminist institution, but I'd had my Smith education and now was ready to graduate and put all that political training to work. In the decade I'd devoted to Smith, there had been a remarkable transformation of American political categories. Half a century after the Great Depression, there was definitely a new moral value assigned to competition, and a far-reaching loss of faith in the capacity of government to engineer the good society. The Vietnam experience as a topic for discussion was a cultural taboo, which left young Americans uncertain that there could be any ethically sound basis for involvement in foreign commitments, creating a kind of isolationism by default. There was also a meaner spirit about the losers in American economic success than had existed since the 1920s.

And the new industrial map of the country arising from offshore production or from effective foreign competition meant a new set of political alignments yet to be understood. I worried about those shifting political forces because I knew the current generation of young women didn't understand how fragile the gains made by my generation really were.

8

SOSTENUTO

❄ I HAD A SUDDEN SHIFT of mood after announcing that I'd finish my term in June 1985. I told the trustees and then the Faculty Council (senate) on a perfect February afternoon just four months ahead of my departure. Then I left the trustees and the faculty group to discuss plans for the search for my successor, and so found myself strolling home unaccustomedly early from a Board afternoon.

I felt both happy and a little lightheaded at my new situation. The customary veil of management preoccupations, which usually prevented me from seeing Smith whole, had vanished. And the disappearance changed my habitual stream of consciousness while I walked across the campus. The usual stream was some version of: What's wrong with the pointing on the brick in that building? People have been parking too close to the roots of that elm. How to stop them without littering the place with signs and fences? Why are those students hanging so far out from that balcony—it's dangerous. Now, for one freshly minted moment, I saw the campus for how beautiful it was. I crossed Elm Street and strolled onto the main campus by John M. Greene Hall. I paused for a moment and looked back to the library and academic buildings, their mellow brick tones luminous in the translucent winter sun. Then I made a right turn to walk along the path between the graceful frame Victorian summer hotels turned Smith student houses, pausing to look down to the steep curve of snow-clad bank that led down to Paradise Pond, thawing now, but in my mind the site of a Currier and Ives scene of students and townspeople skating on the rink prepared daily by Smith's Physical Plant. It was a scene lighted for late-evening skating, and one of my winter joys was to look out about midnight from our house down to the pond, where one or two silent skaters would be performing perfect arabesques, their brightly colored jackets and flashing skates images of the existential joy of such uninhibited and seemingly weightless movement.

Closer to home, I stopped to look at the pre-Revolutionary elm tree whose massive bulk and flying buttresses of trunks had guarded the President's House and its predecessor farmhouse for more than two hundred years. The elm, which had been a young tree at the time of Shay's Rebellion, always reminded me that time has nonhuman dimensions. The elm's baroque pattern of roots, almost half my height, always set my daily affairs in perspective. I always thought of the elm as a very senior professor, since the injections necessary to stave off Dutch elm disease cost annually just about what a chaired professor earned. Today, as I strolled around its roots, it hit me that I was leaving, and that it was going to be harder than I'd thought.

I couldn't walk around the campus without bumping into former faculty assistants, the people I'd lured from classroom, laboratory, and library to work with me on some aspect of the physical campus or some pressing academic plan. As we reminisced, we'd laugh over the pitched battles that had raged over the design of buildings, every passionate protest forgotten as the new structure stood before us, seeming as if it had always been there to new generations of students and faculty.

My plans had all been talked through in confidence with Frances Volkman, the Dean of the Faculty, who was my close working partner in the 1980s. We'd worked out much of the ten-year plan together. A psychologist with a specialty in neuroscience, she'd been the key person to build agreement among science faculty over what new facilities were needed, and how creatively the existing science buildings could be redesigned.

Our conversations now shifted gears to how much of the planning could be carried forward before I left, and how the funding to proceed could be locked in. We'd been a strong team—women of the same academic generation, both married to older academics, both feminists of a highly practical bent. I felt sure we could build the momentum for the science building well before I left, but seeing the doubt in her eyes was an added incentive to get out and begin the fundraising as fast as I could.

Within weeks, we'd begun to block out the calls I had to make, the alumnae gatherings that had to be held to lay the basis of support for the plan, and the case statements and brochures that needed preparation. As we did so, I'd have flashbacks to my arrival a decade ago. I'd been taught fundraising by Smith volunteers, several strong development officers, and one or two excellent consultants. There was now a very efficient machine revving up to make the best use of my time in my last year. It hadn't always been that way. In fact, my legacy to Smith, least visible to outsiders, was a professional fundraising organization and the professional investment process that had been instituted to make the best use of the capital we raised.

The schedule of events planned for me for the next five months set me pondering the paradox of the president's role. It was at once distant, detached, and analytical—and intensely personal. The personal was in the foreground in this period of leavetaking. The other part of the role was largely invisible. My mode of working at the job was three-dimensional; I was a sculptor working on the form and shape of the institution. Because I was concerned with the dynamics of people and place, the design effort resembled a landscaper's work. People, fields of study, and interdisciplinary efforts mature slowly, like trees. Since the enterprise had a relatively simple system of moving financial parts, one had to get the systems working in balance and harmony for real forward momentum, a task requiring engineering talents and lots of persuasion. But once the design and the balanced systems were in place, the institution was carried forward of its own momentum.

When I looked to the future, I still had moments of sheer panic. What if it turned out that I couldn't manage much in life without a sheltering institution? What if John became seriously ill? What if I was totally mistaken about writing as the main theme of my later adulthood? Our entire married life had been lived as custodians of one institution after another. What if we became bored with one another in the long-postponed luxury of private life? What would I do with myself without the discipline of the inexorable schedule? Grandiose plans for midlife mastery of the piano or renewed study of Latin alternated with alarming pictures of a study, a computer, and an empty screen. I shared the most comic anxieties and fantasies with John, but there was no question that what to do was a real puzzle. A puzzle I'd created for myself.

I knew the objective that had brought me to Smith had been realized. Academically strong women's colleges were thriving, and second-tier women's colleges had found many creative ways to expand their mission. Those with life force were safe until the next cultural vogue for questioning self-directing women's institutions. The standard next occupation for a college president was to move on to running a university. What was odd about me was that though there were many enthusiastic invitations, I just didn't want to do that. I'd been working at running academic institutions for the better part of fifteen years. Now I wanted to shift gears.

My aspirations had changed radically while I was at Smith. I'd become disillusioned with professional scholarship as it was lived in the late twentieth century. I had the same vocation to humanistic learning, I still believed in the learned calling, but I wasn't ready to spend my life in department meetings and faculty debates that made the subjects I loved inert and lifeless. There were many humanistic scholars whose work I admired deeply, but most of them had found a way to move beyond disciplinary boundaries and transcend the routine demands of academic life. I'd also reverted to the literary concerns of my undergraduate years and was less deeply invested in history.

I thought the humanities as practiced in the fashion of the day pretty inhumane, concerned with technique rather than meaning, speaking to a smaller and smaller audience. That had happened before. Fashions in scholarship had often been technical and parochial. But the current fashion seemed less about universals and more about political stances on narrowly defined subjects. I knew Shakespeare's plays reflected the gender assumptions of his day. That mattered, but I thought one could recognize the gender questions and move on to the universals about human experience expressed in the tragedies.

I had flashes of insight from postmodern thought, but cultural criticism, though sometimes a valuable field, looked to me like the stamping ground of aging radicals who hadn't managed to win their political goals in the seventies. Fashions in literary criticism seemed to prevent students from taking pleasure in texts, whereas to me the texts had become even more important than in my youth. I would always need them as the tools for building a pattern of meaning out of my life, and as I aged I needed them more urgently than ever.

I felt guilty that I couldn't get stirred up about the culture wars and the way the curriculum had been attacked by the new right in the late eighties. It seemed laughable to me that a curriculum reflecting a growing sense that the Western cultural tradition was not primary but simply one among many great cultures could elicit such spleen. I'd spent enough time in Asia visiting the new Asian tigers and in India exploring the cultures of the Indus Valley that I had not the faintest shadow of uncertainty that the Western tradition must take its place as one among many great visions of mankind, fate, and salvation. It just seemed self-evident to me that given time, the argument would be self-correcting. Just as the railroad and Western weapons had made Europe economically and culturally dominant, the electronically networked world would even the balance. So to me Allan Bloom was just another aging male misogynist, much less gifted than Tertullian or any of a long chain of predecessors.

More comical was the problem that I couldn't settle easily into any of the many thriving women's studies programs that ought to have been a logical home. I was too impatient, even exasperated, with the direction of feminist work in the humanities and social sciences in recent years. Within the Western tradition, there are two possible strategies to follow in arguing for equal treatment of women. The first is to stress their shared rationality with men, and to emphasize the strength of the female body. The second is to argue for compensatory steps to foster equality by assigning new value to women's assumed irrational, emotional, and empathetic selves, and to elevate the social importance of their familial bonds rather than their individuality. I was of the first school, but the dominant vogue of the eighties was the second, to which I was profoundly opposed. So here I was at fifty, a veritable old curmudgeon before my time.

It seemed clear that I would just have to invent my own role and pattern of life, and live it outside the comfortable boundaries of one particular institution. That idea, though bracing, was appealing after living a life hostage to so many constituencies. It would be a shot in the arm to be responsible to no constituencies at all, and speak only for myself. I thought of my fearless parents, creating their rural world without benefit of pensions, health insurance, human resource departments, or counseling services, and decided I would emulate their independence.

My plan was to divide my life into thirds. I'd spend part of it learning to become a writer, and working on creating a counter record to the feminist ideas I thought so mistaken. I'd write about what women were not supposed to acknowledge—ambition, love of adventure, the quest for intellectual power, physical courage and endurance, risk taking, the negative aspects of mother/daughter relations always so relentlessly sentimentalized. And I'd write about it in some other literary form than the stereotypical romance.

I'd spend part of my time learning how to think about the environmental issues that had personal meaning for me from my childhood in semi-arid Australia. I thought the ecofeminist worldview, which located all environmental damage in male aggressiveness, about on a par with the fantasies of eighteenth-century marginal sects who expected Christ to return in female form. They were both instances of the ideologies of the disempowered, but they were not paths to effective action. I had only to listen to the diminishing bird sounds in my Conway woods, however, or look at the ash trees and elms ceasing to thrive, to know that the biosphere was changing in response to human depredations. Because I'd lived a good slice of life without electric power, indoor plumbing, or, during 1940–45, gasoline, I didn't idealize preindustrial society the way urban environmentalists did. Instead I wanted to understand the political, social, and cultural arrangements that could reduce the draw on the environment yet retain most of the benefits created by machine technology. That was the reason for the part-time affiliation I arranged at MIT's Program in Science, Technology, and Society. I'd go back to being a student and professor there, enjoy wonderful colleagues and students, but never have to argue again about another appointment.

I'd spend a third of my time helping to govern institutions I wasn't responsible for running. Corporations, foundations, hospitals, schools, colleges. That would keep me in touch with the business world, higher education, and the social causes I cared about. But I'd report to no one, and I'd be as free to explore the world with John as we had been when we were first married.

I hoped that in that new pattern of life I'd get back to the self squeezed out by the daily schedule, the rush from plane or helicopter, to waiting car, to next meeting, to formal dinner. I'd cook in my own kitchen again and plant my own bulbs. John and I could read to one another again in the evenings, and I'd be responsible only to the self who'd become something of a stranger.

A symbol of the leavetaking was sitting for the obligatory presidential portrait. I asked the trustees in charge to find a woman portrait artist, someone young and promising, not the already successful, and therefore possibly formulaic, practitioner. The assignment brought me an unexpected gift, because conversations during sittings with Sarah Swenson, the portrait artist chosen, opened up for me what an intensely visual person I was and launched a set of relationships with working artists that became one of the delights of my next phase in life.

My portrait was to preside over the Sophia Smith Collection, the priceless Smith archive of women's history that would shape how future scholars understood American women's lives and institutions. I'd begun working there as a beginning graduate student in 1960, astonished that America had such scholarly investment in the history of women. It's a marking point in life when one begins to preside in effigy. And it's even more so when the place brings to mind a much younger self. I loved the portrait. I thought Sarah really got me on the canvas.

But seeing it hung was something of a shock. I was used to studying the portraits in libraries, hospital foyers, school assembly rooms, and college administration buildings to decipher the iconography of a place, but I wasn't prepared to see myself there. I couldn't help looking at it with the skeptical eye I'd turned on other such figures. This image was timeless, and I would be traveling away from it and becoming another person in the process. It was interesting to speculate about what one would think of the other in twenty-five years. And then what would future generations of Jill Conway—like visitors make of the image on the wall? It was like an infinite regression of mirrors and made me slightly dizzy.

John retired a year before we left Smith without the slightest tremor of uncertainty about the future. When we settled back in Boston, he wanted to read theology, renew old friendships, and volunteer for serious work with a Catholic charity. After we found the ideal house, with a tranquil library looking out on a romantic garden, the plan was complete. We'd light the fire there on snowy afternoons and relish the life together given back to us by his escape from the unknown disease of the nerve endings that had come close to leaving him paralyzed.

As for me, I was accustomed to thinking about life in the language of music and I couldn't quite determine which part of the symphony I was in. Was it going to be a rousing third movement? or a somber but reconciling fourth? Whatever it was, I knew I had to concentrate on getting the opening chords right, because those are the ones one never gets to play a second time.

Acknowledgments

I am indebted to Elizabeth Kennan, Sarah Doering, Stephen and Margaret Graubard, Susan Bourque, and Leo and Jane Marx for reading many early drafts of this book. Their advice was invaluable, as was that of Jane Garrett, my editor at Alfred A. Knopf, and Luann Walther, my editor at Vintage Books. Amber Watt was an indefatigable researcher, helping to track down dates, documents, and photographs to help fill the blanks in my memory. The staff of the Smith College archives was always generous with innumerable requests for help. Debbie Federico, Bernadette Fossa, and Joan Frohock kept track of the manuscript and of my punctuation.

BOOKS BY JILL KER CONWAY

THE ROAD FROM COORAIN

The Road from Coorain is Jill Ker Conway's clear-sighted memoir of growing up Australian: from the vastness of a sheep station in the outback to the stifling propriety of postwar Sydney; from an untutored childhood to a life in academia; and from the shelter of a protective family to the lessons of independence. In this exceptional memoir, Conway creates a magnificently vivid portrait of coming of age in mid-century Australia.

Autobiography/0-679-72436-2

TRUE NORTH

In this second volume of her memoirs, Jill Ker Conway sets off for America, where she becomes a renowned historian and, later, the first woman president of Smith College. This is a story of intellectual discovery, as Conway enters a lively community of female scholars, and it is the story of a love affair that ripened into a remarkable marriage. Written with elegance and verve, *True North* examines the challenges that confront all women who seek to establish public selves and reconcile them with their private passions.

Memoir/Women's Studies/0-679-74461-4

WHEN MEMORY SPEAKS
Exploring the Art of Autobiography

In recent years, the memoir has been both celebrated as our liveliest literary genre and condemned as the confessional mode of a self-obsessed society. Jill Ker Conway, the widely acclaimed author of a bestselling memoir, has written an astute book about the memoir form itself—discussing some of the most notable examples of the genre, from St. Teresa of Avila and Jean-Jacques Rousseau to Frank McCourt and Katharine Graham.

Literary Criticism/Essays/0-679-76645-6

IN HER OWN WORDS
Women's Memoirs from Australia, New Zealand, Canada, and the United States

In this collection, we meet twelve extraordinary women, from Shirley Chisholm, the West Indian-raised girl who became the first black woman elected to Congress, to Janet Frame, the New Zealand writer who overcame involuntary treatment in a mental institution to write one of the archetypal analyses of the postcolonial experience. *In Her Own Words* is a brilliant distillation of women's political and private experiences in the four offshoots of the old British world.

Autobiography/Women's Studies/0-679-78153-6

WRITTEN BY HERSELF
Autobiographies of American Women: An Anthology

Written by Herself presents an affecting and thoughtful anthology of American women's autobiographical writing, from Jane Addams and Zora Neale Hurston to Gloria Steinem and Maxine Hong Kingston. Whether the narrator is Maya Angelou or Margaret Mead, these voices resonate in their candor, passion, and unflinching self-awareness.

Autobiography/Women's Studies/0-679-73633-6

WRITTEN BY HERSELF, VOLUME II
Women's Memoirs from Britain, Africa, Asia, and the United States: An Anthology

The women who tell their stories in this volume represent three generations, four continents, and an unequaled range of experience, from England's Vera Brittain to South Africa's Emma Mashinini and from Vijaya Lakshmi Pandit of India to American Edith Mirante. These intelligent and instructive models demonstrate the ways in which women everywhere strive for power, inclusion, and autonomy.

Autobiography/Women's Studies/0-679-75109-2